# *The Official NASCAR Busch Series Handbook*

## THE OFFICIAL NASCAR BUSCH SERIES HANDBOOK

Other NASCAR Books Available:

**NASCAR 50: The Thunder of America**
**NASCAR Cooks**
**Official NASCAR Trivia**
**The Official NASCAR Winston Cup Series Handbook**
**Jeff Gordon, Portrait of a Champion**
**NASCAR 50 Greatest Drivers**
**NASCAR Trials & Triumphs**

# The Official NASCAR Busch Series Handbook

*Everything You Want*

*to Know about the*

*NASCAR Busch Series,*

*Grand National Division*

HarperEntertainment

*A Division of* HarperCollins*Publishers*

HarperCollins books may be purchased for educational, business, or sales promotional use. For information please write: Special Markets Department, HarperCollins Publishers Inc., 10 East 53rd Street, New York, NY 10022–5299.

FIRST EDITION

© 1998 Anheuser-Busch, Inc., Busch Beer, St. Louis, MO

Photography by Street & Smith Sports Group and Daytona Racing Archives.

Designed by Christina Bliss, Staten Island, NY

**Library of Congress Cataloging-in-Publication Data**

The official NASCAR Busch series handbook : everything you want to
   know about the NASCAR Busch Series, Grand National Division/NASCAR.—1st ed.
      p.   cm.
   ISBN 0–06–107332–6
   1. Stock car racing—United States.  I. NASCAR (Association)
GV1029.9.S740367  1999                        99-11063
796.72'0973—dc21

99 00 01 02 03  10 9 8 7 6 5 4 3 2 1

# CONTENTS

# *INTRODUCTION*

So you want to learn about the NASCAR Busch Series, Grand National Division? Whether you're a long-time fan of the series, or a relative newcomer, this book is the ultimate guide for you.

*The Official NASCAR Busch Series Handbook: Everything You Want to Know About the NASCAR Busch Series, Grand National Division* gives you an insider's look at the second-most-popular form of motorsports in the U.S.

You'll find everything you need to know about the series within the pages of this book. From the birth of the NASCAR Busch Series, to its heroes, its rookies, its cars, and its races, this handbook will give you the most in-depth analysis available, focusing on the series' size, scope, and competition. The NASCAR Busch Series continues to attract new fans every day. Now, even newcomers can speak as knowl-

edgeably about the series as those who've been fans since the series' inception.

So, sit back, relax, and get ready for one of the most exciting rides you'll experience.

This handbook takes you through the history of the series up to the end of the 1998 season. We've separated the book into six easy-to-read sections so you can read it all at once, or flip to the sections that most interest you.

In Part One we take a look back at the evolution of the NASCAR Busch Series. The NASCAR Busch Series was born in 1982 when NASCAR consolidated the Late Model Sportsman Division. With the help of the series' title sponsor, Anheuser-Busch, the series' growth has been unstoppable ever since. We'll give you a look at the drivers who made the series successful in those early years, and the ones who are doing the same today.

In Part Two we'll get your engines warmed up. We'll describe each of the members of a racing crew and explain their responsibilities. You'll also learn about the dynamics of a pit stop, qualifying for a race, and NASCAR official inspections.

Part Three gets you in the car and on the track. We'll take an up-close look at a NASCAR Busch Series race car, checking out the car's body and under the hood. We'll compare it to a NASCAR Winston Cup Series car, and you'll see how the cars are alike and different. Then, it's time to get on the track. Ever wonder why there are single-file and double-file restarts? Or how a driver knows when there's a caution, or when to pit? After you read this section you'll be just as knowledgeable as the drivers themselves.

Then, it's time for payday. Every driver on the track strives for the same goal: victory lane. We'll take you to victory lane and let you feel the excitement of winning. We'll also explain the NASCAR Busch Series point distribution and the series championship.

But, that's not all. There's also a handy guide in the back of the book that provides you with the addresses of your favorite drivers as well as NASCAR publications and radio and television shows. And lastly, a detailed glossary is included so you never have to stumble over a word again.

This handbook was authorized by NASCAR, so you can be sure everything included is factual and true. Written by NASCAR's competition department and a veteran NASCAR Busch Series writer, Bill Kiser, this handbook will become the basis of your NASCAR Busch Series knowledge.

So, take the time and enjoy learning everything you can about one of the most popular forms of motorsports in the U.S. Once you've read *The Official NASCAR Busch Series Handbook: Everything You Want to Know About the NASCAR Busch Series, Grand National Division*, you'll be ready to head to your local NASCAR track.

PART ONE: *Evolution of the NASCAR Busch Series*

CHAPTER ONE

# THE BIRTH OF A SERIES

When the green flag dropped to start the 1999 NAPA 300 at Daytona International Speedway, it marked the beginning of the 18th season of the NASCAR Busch Series, Grand National Division's existence. But while the series is relatively young compared to its big brother, the NASCAR Winston Cup Series, its roots go deep into NASCAR's fifty years of existence.

## -------How Did It All Get Started?

Automobile racing has been around almost as long as the automobile itself, but stock car racing didn't begin to surface until after the Second World War, during the surge toward economic prosperity in the United States, with the automobile as its central symbol.

During World War II all U.S. auto factories, and the materials needed to build cars, had been converted or diverted to military uses. As a result, from 1942 to 1946 there were virtually no new cars built. Once the war was over, however, and the millions of soldiers, sailors, and airmen who fought returned home from Europe and the Pacific, they brought with them a tremendous demand for new cars.

As the domestic automobile makers began to produce cars again, it was inevitable that men would race them. In postwar America, the newer automobile designs rolling out of the factories were faster and more powerful than ever. And drivers wanted to race the cars that you could buy from local dealers, not the more costly, custom-built racers that competed at Indianapolis Motor Speedway and other tracks.

In some regions of the country there was a particularly intense passion for racing.

Foreign and sports cars running road courses were big on the West Coast, while open wheelers such as sprint and midget cars running on dirt tracks were popular in the Midwest. In the Southeast, the racing passion was in production-based American cars. Along those lines, tales were being spread about moonshiners—young drivers racing up and down the back roads of the South in souped-up cars, delivering loads of illegally produced liquor.

Of course, it was inevitable that some of the moonshiners would butt heads over who had the fastest cars. Sometimes their arguments would be settled on the track, sometimes off it.

Local racetrack promoters saw the potential to turn this largely regional passion into a national sport, and not surprisingly, a lot of people wanted in on the action. The widespread interest led to the creation of dozens of organizations that professed to represent stock car racing.

Among the many sanctioning bodies that were formed in the late 1940s were the National Championship Stock Car Circuit, or NCSCC; the Stock Car Auto Racing Society, which carried the uncomfortable acronym SCARS; the National Stock Car Racing Association (NSCRA); the United Stock Car Racing Association (USCRA); and the National Auto Racing League (NARL).

Just about anybody with access to a racetrack and drivers formed their own local sanctioning body, or so it seemed. And what with every circuit and sanctioning body having its own "champion," getting media coverage—mainly from newspapers and radio—proved nearly impossible, because it was difficult for sports reporters and editors

to ascertain who the real champions were. It was apparent that unifying stock car racing was vital to the sport's success.

The man who set out to bring this about was Bill France Sr., known as "Big Bill" to the racing community.

France had promoted and even raced in events under the NSCRA and SCARS organizations, but wanted to put together a true unified national stock car series. With the stated goal of forming a national sanctioning body to run stock car racing, France convened a meeting of thirty-five of automobile racing's most influential people on December 14, 1947, at the Streamline Hotel in Daytona Beach, Florida.

The group spent four days discussing and crafting rules and regulations that would determine how the sport would be operated. And from that meeting, a new stock car sanctioning body was formed: NASCAR, which stood for the National Association of Stock Car Auto Racing, a title that has generally been credited to famed mechanic Red Vogt. Its first race was run on February 14, 1948, and NASCAR was incorporated on February 21, 1948, with France elected president.

## -------The Early Years

With a shortage of new cars, NASCAR's inaugural season consisted of mostly prewar models racing in a class called "Modifieds," a series that still exists to this day. In 1948, NASCAR ran a 52-race Modified schedule, with Red Byron winning the series championship.

The next year, France's plans for a "strictly stock" division—the precursor of the NASCAR Winston Cup Series—came into being. As the name suggests, the cars literally were stock cars, with no modifications allowed.

The first NASCAR Strictly Stock event was a 200-lap race held at the now-defunct Charlotte Speedway in Charlotte, North Carolina. It brought with it 33 cars, about 13,000 spectators, a $5,000 guaranteed purse, the very first rules controversy in NASCAR history, and the first chapter in the NASCAR legend.

The race was won by Glenn Dunnaway in a 1947 Ford he'd set up to haul moonshine, but it was determined afterward that the car had illegal rear springs—a common modification among those hauling sour mash and outrunning federal agents in those days—so Dunnaway was disqualified and the victory was given to Jim Roper and his 1949 Mercury, which he'd driven cross-country to compete in the first strictly stock NASCAR race.

*The NASCAR Busch Series, Grand National Division actually got its start as the NASCAR Late Model Sportsman Division. The sportsman division was converted into the NASCAR Busch Series in 1982.*

The NASCAR Strictly Stock Division would hold eight races during the 1949 season, with Byron once again winning the championship, ahead of Lee Petty and Bob Flock.

## -------What About the NASCAR Busch Series?

The forerunner of the NASCAR Busch Series, Grand National Division was the NASCAR Late Model Sportsman Division, which sprang into existence in 1950, just two years after "Big Bill" began running what has become one of the world's most successful racing operations.

While the then-NASCAR Grand National Series (now known as the NASCAR Winston Cup Series) garnered most of the attention, with many of its top drivers becoming stars, the NASCAR Late Model Sportsman Division grew its own crop of name drivers.

Among those who won NASCAR Late Model Sportsman national championships

were, in 1956, the late Ralph Earnhardt, the father of seven-time NASCAR Winston Cup Series champion Dale Earnhardt; Ned Jarrett, in 1957–58, the father of current NASCAR Winston Cup Series driver Dale Jarrett; Rene Charland, who won four consecutive titles between 1962 and 1965; and Red Farmer, whose three straight championships in 1969–71 made him a well-known member of the "Alabama Gang."

These drivers, and many more like them, made their names racing on short tracks—often called "bullrings" because of their size—up and down the East Coast. Running sixty or seventy races during a season, sometimes more, became commonplace for the top NASCAR Late Model Sportsman teams, with drivers and crew often running three or four races a week, driving all night to get to the next event.

"Some years, I'd run sixty to sixty-five races a year," said Tommy Houston, one of the NASCAR Late Model Sportsman Division's top drivers. "We could race on Thursday, then take the same car somewhere else on Friday night, then run it again on Saturday and Sunday nights.

"If we had a track to run on, and someone said they were gonna have a race that night, then we'd be there. That's what we were doing—we were racing. It wasn't one of these deals where we needed to take backup cars, but we did take spare engines. We'd use the same car, and if we crashed it or had a problem, we'd beat it out and fix it, then go on and race again."

By the late 1970s and early 1980s, drivers who wanted to run for the national NASCAR Late Model Sportsman championship would fly or drive to dozens of tracks in the course

Tommy Houston was one of the many drivers who stayed with the NASCAR Busch Series after its evolution from the NASCAR Late Model Sportsman Division. He still holds many records in the series, including most consecutive starts: 360.

of a season, often calling ahead to find a local team willing to field them a car, or driving all night to get to the next race.

For example, on Labor Day weekend in 1973, three-time NASCAR Late Model Sportsman champ Jack Ingram ran six races in a five-day span: a 200-lap race in South Carolina, a 250-lap race in Maryland, 300-lap races in Virginia and in Tennessee, a 500-lap race in Minnesota, and a 200-lap race in Tennessee again, the last two on the same day.

It was that kind of schedule, along with the expense of doing it, that brought about a major change in 1982. NASCAR's top officials, taking the same step they made a decade earlier with the now-named

Jack Ingram was a three-time champion during the series NASCAR Late Model Sportsman division and a champion twice more under the series NASCAR Busch Series, Grand National Division title.

NASCAR Winston Cup Series, consolidated the NASCAR Late Model Sportsman Division into a touring series, running 29 races its first season.

"The biggest thing was to try to provide an avenue for one of our biggest divisions and some of our biggest stars," said Kevin Triplett, NASCAR's director of operations. "In 1982, in certain parts of the country, some of the stars of the NASCAR Late Model Sportsman Division were as popular as NASCAR Winston Cup drivers. Jack Ingram, Tommy Ellis, Tommy Houston, Sam Ard,

*In 1982, NASCAR consolidated the Late Model Sportsman division into a touring series; it consisted of only 29 races during its first year.*

guys like that were very popular, and a lot of the races they ran and racetracks they ran, when you took it as a whole and looked at it, it provided an opportunity for a good series in itself.

"Instead of racing at different racetracks for points, where it was pretty much the same guys every week, it provided an avenue for another national series. Some people may argue about how long it took to become a national series, but we always considered it that from the beginning."

The first race of the new NASCAR Budweiser Late Model Sportsman Series (which changed its name several years later to the current NASCAR Busch Series, Grand National Division) was held February 13,

*Sam Ard was a back-to-back series champion in 1983 and 1984.*

1982, at Daytona International Speedway, with West Virginian Mike Porter winning the series first-ever pole position, and Dale Earnhardt—two years after winning the first of his seven NASCAR Winston Cup Series championships—winning the race.

The early years of the NASCAR Busch Series, Grand National Division were dominated by the veterans from the NASCAR Late Model Sportsman Division, who used their knowledge of the short tracks the series primarily ran. In addition, the competitors could take the time to focus on the reduced number of tracks and prepare their own equipment for each race.

"It was a blessing to be able to race in a series where you knew where you were going to go from the fall when the schedule was sent out," said Ingram, who won seven races in 1982 en route to winning the inaugural NASCAR Busch Series, Grand National Division championship.

The battle for that first title came down to the last race of the season, with Ingram beating out Ard (a four-race winner in '82) by just 49 points for the championship.

That championship battle set the stage for the NASCAR Busch Series, Grand National Division's fledgling years. Ard would come back to win the championship in 1983, setting a still-held series record for wins in a season with ten, then becoming the first repeat champion with an eight-victory season in '84. Ingram would become the series second repeat titlist when he won five races and the series championship in 1985.

The beginning of NASCAR's ultimate plan—to have the NASCAR Busch Series, Grand National Division serve as a stepping-stone to the NASCAR Winston Cup Series—came about in 1986 when Larry Pearson, the oldest son of star driver David Pearson, won the first of his back-to-back championships.

Even though Tommy Ellis became the last of the NASCAR Late Model Sportsman Division's star to win the NASCAR Busch Series, Grand

*Larry Pearson, No. 21, and Jimmy Hensley, No. 5, were strong contenders during the early years of the series.*

National Division title (in 1988), the youth movement began in earnest in the late 1980s when the late Rob Moroso won the series championship in 1989 at age twenty-one.

Pearson was the first NASCAR Busch Series, Grand National Division champion to make the jump to the NASCAR Winston Cup Series. Moroso made the move in 1990, but was killed in an automobile accident later that year and was awarded the series rookie-of-the-year title posthumously.

Others have also made the move since then, and most are still in the NASCAR Winston Cup Series, which counts former NASCAR Busch Series, Grand National Division champions Bobby Labonte (1991), Joe Nemechek (1992), Steve Grissom (1993),

David Green (1994), and Johnny Benson (1995) among its current active roster.

In fact, in the past decade seven drivers who made their names in the NASCAR Busch Series, Grand National Division went on to win the NASCAR Winston Cup Series rookie-of-the-year title: Moroso (1990), Bobby Hamilton (1991), Jimmy Hensley (1992), Jeff Gordon (1993)—in a class that also included current drivers Bobby Labonte and Kenny Wallace—Jeff Burton (1994), Ricky Craven (1995), and Benson (1996).

Randy LaJoie became the fourth driver in NASCAR Busch Series, Grand National Division history to win more than one series championship, and just the third to win back-to-back titles, taking the prize in 1996 and 1997, and setting records along the way for season and career winnings. In 1997 the Norwalk, Connecticut, native became the first driver in series history to win more than $1 million in a season, pocketing $1,105,201 in race winnings and postseason bonuses, more than double his take from his previous championship season.

*ABOVE LEFT: Joe Nemechek, one of the many NASCAR Busch Series drivers to make the move to the NASCAR Winston cup Series, was the series 1992 champion. BELOW: Randy LaJoie, driving the No.74 Chevrolet Monte Carlo, became the first driver to win more than $1 million in season winnings. He did so with the second of his two consecutive championships in 1997.*

Third-generation driver Dale Earnhardt Jr. claimed the NASCAR Busch Series title in 1998, his rookie season in the series.

*Casey Atwood, left, and Adam Petty are two members of the younger generation making their mark in the NASCAR Busch Series.*

*Jack Ingram won $122,100 in race winnings and postseason bonuses by claiming victory in the inaugural NASCAR Budweiser Late Model Sportsman Series championship in 1982. Since then, in the NASCAR Busch Series, Grand National Division, race winnings and postseason bonuses have increased enormously. In 1998, Dale Earnhardt Jr. won a total of $1,332,701.*

## -------The Next Generation

NASCAR's "next generation" made its presence felt in 1998, with Dale Earnhardt Jr. joining his famous grandfather and more famous father as a NASCAR champion when he won the NASCAR Busch Series, Grand National Division title, winning a tour-high seven races and over $800,000 in race winnings.

While the youngest champion in the Earnhardt clan also has plans to move to the NASCAR Winston Cup Series ranks, that won't happen until the year 2000. He's back to defend his NASCAR Busch Series, Grand National Division championship in 1999, taking on the challenge from such drivers as former champions LaJoie, Pearson, and Chuck Bown (1990), and up-and-coming drivers such as Matt Kenseth and Mike McLaughlin.

The third and even fourth generations of racing families are making their presence felt in the NASCAR Busch Series, Grand National Division as well. In addition to the youngest Earnhardt, his older brother Kerry Earnhardt is also a series regular; and the sons of current and former drivers such as Adam Petty (grandson of Richard and son of Kyle), Barry Bodine (son of Geoff), Jason Jarrett (grandson of Ned and son of Dale), and Bobby Hamilton Jr. (son of Bobby Hamilton), will all run NASCAR Busch Series events in 1999.

CHAPTER TWO

# MILESTONES IN SERIES HISTORY

The transition of the NASCAR Late Model Sportsman Division from its Gypsy-caravan-like roots to the modern day phenomenon that is the NASCAR Busch Series, Grand National Division wouldn't have taken place without the backing of a major corporate partner.

NASCAR found such a partner in Anheuser-Busch, one of the world's largest brewing companies, which had become involved in motor sports in the late 1970s and was looking to expand.

Anheuser-Busch first became involved in NASCAR in 1978, when it backed the Busch Pole Award program on the NASCAR Winston Cup Series. It then sponsored the Busch Clash, now known as the Bud Shootout, an annual event at Daytona International Speedway that pits the pole winners from the previous season against each other in a 25-lap dash.

The brewing company, based in St. Louis, Missouri, stepped up to the NASCAR plate again in 1982 when the NASCAR Late Model Sportsman Division underwent its transition, backing what was called the NASCAR Budweiser Late Model Sportsman Series in a 29-race schedule its inaugural season.

*Anheuser-Busch has since expanded its involvement in NASCAR, not only by its increased sponsorship of the NASCAR Busch Series, Grand National Division and NASCAR's Bud Pole Award for the three national touring series— the NASCAR Winston Cup Series; the NASCAR Busch Series, Grand National Division; and the NASCAR Craftsman Truck Series—but by also sponsoring the*

*Busch North Series and the Busch All-Star Series, both part of the NASCAR Touring Division. The Busch North Series is a sister division that races primarily on short and intermediate tracks in the northeastern United States, and the NASCAR Busch All-Star Tour is the only dirt-track racing series still sanctioned by NASCAR.*

## --------Changing Names

The series underwent its first major title change in 1984 when Anheuser-Busch switched its sponsorship from its Budweiser brand, one of the best-selling beer brands in the world, to its Busch brand. At the same time, another NASCAR touring series—the NASCAR Winston Cup Series—dropped "Grand National" from its title. It didn't disappear, however—with the new sponsorship, NASCAR renamed the NASCAR Budweiser Late Model Sportsman Series the NASCAR Busch Grand National Series, or as it was commonly called by competitors and race fans across the country, BGN.

*When the NASCAR Budweiser Late Model Sportsman Series was formed in 1982, it primarily stuck with its roots. Since most of the old NASCAR Late Model Sportsman Division events were run on short tracks, the new series followed suit. Of the 29 races held in '82, just six were run on speedways—tracks of one mile or more.*

"The name Grand National has been involved in NASCAR since the beginning," Kevin Triplett, NASCAR's director of operations, said. "Bill [France] Sr. felt that 'Grand' and 'National' were two words together that described exactly what he was trying to do—a grand racing series on a national basis."

The title changes—there have only been three in the series seventeen-year history—also came at a time when the series itself was undergoing major changes, both on and off the track.

## --------Jumping on the Bandwagon

But as the series developed a following, more and more speedways began jumping on the speedway bandwagon, most using it as a support event for the NASCAR Winston Cup Series races. By 1992 speedways were as prevalent as short tracks—there were fifteen of each, plus one road course, on that year's 31-event schedule. Since then, the NASCAR Busch Series, Grand National Division has become almost a mirror image of its big brother, with 21 of 31 events run on speedways last year.

The transition from a short-track series to a speedway-based division began in 1992 when three major speedway events were added at Talladega Superspeedway, Michigan Speedway, and Atlanta Motor Speedway. The changes continued in the following years with the additions of such venues as The Milwaukee Mile and the Miami-Dade Homestead Motorsports Complex, the first time a NASCAR touring series event had been held in South Florida.

*Hickory Motor Speedway is one of the original short tracks on the series. It has been dropped from the schedule due to the series growth into larger markets.*

*Hickory Motor Speedway, which has hosted NASCAR touring division events since the track was built in the 1950s, has been the site of more NASCAR Busch Series, Grand National Division events than any other track. Since 1982, the .363-mile Hickory, North Carolina, "bullring" has staged 41 NASCAR Busch Series events.*

The year 1995 also brought about the current title: the NASCAR Busch Series, Grand National Division.

In 1997, the series took another leap forward, with the addition of four new race-

tracks to the schedule, three of them west of the Mississippi River and the fourth right on its eastern banks. Joining the NASCAR Busch Series, Grand National Division were the California Speedway, the Las Vegas Motor Speedway, the Texas Motor Speedway, and Gateway International Raceway (Madison, Illinois), all brand-new tracks, three of which could seat more than 100,000 race fans.

In 1998, NASCAR added a fourth event west of the Mississippi River, putting the brand new Pike's Peak International Raceway

In 1997, the series made a move west and raced for the first time at Las Vegas Motor Speedway.

decade. Television ratings have also grown, outpacing most other racing series and sitting on a par with sports such as professional golf, major league baseball, and the National Basketball Association.

*Speedways were nothing new to the drivers of the old NASCAR Late Model Sportsman Division, the predecessor of today's NASCAR Busch Series, Grand National Division. Late Model Sportsman events had been held for years at tracks such as Daytona International Speedway, Charlotte Motor Speedway, North Carolina Speedway, and Dover Downs International Speedway.*

on the schedule. In 1999 there will be a fifth race in the West—at Phoenix International Raceway—joining the roster of host tracks.

But despite the growth of the NASCAR Busch Series, Grand National Division to bigger, better, and faster racetracks across the country, the series still holds on to its weekly short-track roots. For 1999, short-track NASCAR Busch Series events have been scheduled at South Boston Speedway, Virginia; Myrtle Beach Speedway; Indianapolis Raceway Park; Richmond (Virginia) International Raceway; the Bristol Motor Speedway and Nashville Speedway USA, in Tennessee; and a new event at the Memphis Motorsports Park.

With this expansion and the changes that have occurred along the way, the NASCAR Busch Series, Grand National Division has become the second-most-attended racing series in the United States. It has grown a phenomenal 286 percent over the past

## Stepping Back

With more and more NASCAR Busch Series events being held in conjunction with the NASCAR Winston Cup Series—21 of 32 races in 1999—more drivers from NASCAR's top series are being attracted to run NASCAR Busch Series events.

Probably the most successful of those has been Mark Martin, who put together an impressive string of wins over the past several years with his Roush Racing NASCAR Busch Series, Grand National Division team.

Martin, a four-time American Speed Association champion, had tried to run the NASCAR Winston Cup Series in the early 1980s, only to run out of luck and money. He

Although a full-time contender on the NASCAR Winston Cup Series, Mark Martin holds the NASCAR Busch Series record for most wins.

returned to the Midwest-based ASA tour briefly, then hooked up with team owner Bruce Lawmaster to run the full NASCAR Busch Series schedule in 1987.

The Batesville, Arkansas, native won three races that season and finished eighth in the NASCAR Busch Series point standings, but he also drew the attention of fledging NASCAR Winston Cup Series team owner Jack Roush, who had campaigned championship-winning teams on the road racing circuits but was looking to expand into stock car racing.

The rest, as they say, is history—not only have Martin and Roush become one of the most formidable teams in NASCAR Winston Cup Series history, but they have also put together a stellar NASCAR Busch Series program as well, winning races almost at will over the past five years.

Their most impressive win of all came late in the 1997 season, on October 25, when Martin broke Jack Ingram's all-time NASCAR Busch Series, Grand National Division victory record at North Carolina Motor Speedway in Rockingham. Martin's victory over Roush Racing teammate Jeff Burton gave him his 32nd career NASCAR Busch Series, Grand National Division win, surpassing Ingram's career record of 31 victories.

"I still say this isn't anything compared to what Jack Ingram did," said Martin, who has since added another victory to his NASCAR Busch Series record. "It took me ten years to do what he did in five. It doesn't really compare, but it feels good. We've won a lot of races, and this was a hard-fought one today. We've had some lucky ones this year…but this one we had to earn."

*Last year, drivers from the NASCAR Winston Cup Series claimed just ten victories in 31 NASCAR Busch Series, Grand National Division races. The NASCAR Winston Cup Series contingent was led by Jeff Burton, who won three times; Joe Nemechek, who won twice; and Jimmy Spencer, Bobby Labonte, Mark Martin, Kevin Lepage, and Dick Trickle, who won one race each.*

## --------Records, Records, Records

Martin isn't the only driver to hold a record in the NASCAR Busch Series, Grand National Division. Others include:

**Tommy Houston:** The Hickory, North Carolina, native, one of the crossover drivers from the old NASCAR Late Model Sportsman Division, showed longevity in the NASCAR Busch Series, Grand National Division. He currently holds the series records for most career starts (417), most consecutive starts (360), and most top-five (123) and top–10 finishes (198) in a career.

**Jack Ingram:** Despite losing the career victories record to Mark Martin, Ingram still holds his share of NASCAR Busch Series, Grand National Division records, including most career short-track wins (29), most wins at one track (eight, at Hickory Motor Speedway), and most consecutive wins at one track (five, at South Boston Speedway).

*Jack Ingram still holds several records in the NASCAR Busch Series, Grand National Division. However, Mark Martin recently broke his record for most series wins.*

**Sam Ard:** The two-time NASCAR Busch Series, Grand National Division champion had his racing career cut short by an accident in 1985, but he still holds such series records as most races won from the pole position in a season (four, in 1983) and career (nine), most top-five (twenty-four) and top–ten finishes (thirty) in a season, and most consecutive races running at the finish (forty-six, from July 1983 to October 1984).

**Tommy Ellis:** Another crossover driver from the NASCAR Late Model Sportsman Division, where he won the last series title in 1981 before the series changed to the NASCAR Busch Series, Grand National Division. Ellis won the championship in 1988 and still holds the series record for pole positions won in a career (twenty-eight).

**Jeff Gordon:** Before Gordon jumped into the national spotlight with his three NASCAR Winston Cup Series championships, he made his mark on the NASCAR Busch Series, Grand National Division record book by setting a record for most pole positions won in a season (eleven, in 1992).

**Dale Earnhardt:** While Earnhardt is best known for his seven NASCAR Winston Cup Series championships, he also holds NASCAR Busch Series, Grand

ABOVE: Dale Earnhardt holds a NASCAR Busch Series record of most consecutive wins at one track.

BELOW: Dick Trickle is best known as the series oldest race winner. Trickle won his record-breaking race at the age of 55 years and five months.

National Division records for most consecutive years winning at least one race (ten, from 1985 to 1994), and most consecutive wins at one track (five, at Daytona International Speedway).

***Dick Trickle:*** This veteran late model driver got a late start on the NASCAR scene, but has since made up for it by becoming the NASCAR Busch Series, Grand National Division's oldest race winner. When he won the Galaxy Foods 300 at Hickory Motor Speedway March 29, 1997, Trickle was fifty-five years, five months old.

***Ed Berrier:*** The Winston-Salem, North Carolina, native held one of the NASCAR Busch Series, Grand National Division's least-wanted records: most starts without a win. After his first NASCAR Busch Series start in 1984, Berrier went 208 starts without a win, with his best finish a second place at South Boston Speedway in 1987. But that streak ended on his 209th career start, when Berrier won at Hickory Motor Speedway last year.

***Johnny Rumley:*** This journeyman racer, who had kicked around NASCAR Winston Racing Series weekly short tracks for years, set a NASCAR Busch Series, Grand National Division record when he posted his first series victory in just his seventh career start. That win also came at Hickory Motor Speedway on November 7, 1993, in a race car that he and several friends had put together. Rumley has since gone on to win another NASCAR Busch Series event, at Dover Downs International Speedway in 1995.

# CHAPTER THREE

## NASCAR'S PROVING GROUND

**W**hen NASCAR officials decided to consolidate the NASCAR Late Model Sportsman Division into what is now the NASCAR Busch Series, Grand National Division, one of the goals was to give the NASCAR Winston Cup Series a "proving ground" for new drivers.

The goal succeeded beyond the wildest expectations. Today, a majority of the drivers running the NASCAR Winston Cup Series circuit can trace their roots back to the NASCAR Busch Series, and some are even left from the old NASCAR Late Model Sportsman Division.

Tops among the "graduates" from the NASCAR Busch Series are three-time NASCAR Winston Cup Series champion Jeff Gordon, former NASCAR Busch Series champs Johnny Benson, David Green, Steve Grissom, Bobby Labonte, and Joe Nemechek; Jeff and Ward Burton, Dale Jarrett, Mark Martin, Bobby

Hamilton, Jimmy Spencer, Chad Little, Steve Park, Brett and Geoff Bodine, Kenny Wallace, Robert Pressley, Rick Mast, and Kevin Lepage.

As for the NASCAR Late Model Sportsman veterans, count seven-time NASCAR Winston Cup Series champion Dale Earnhardt and four-time race winner Morgan Shepherd among them.

**PIT STOP** *Dale Earnhardt also has his name in the NASCAR Busch Series, Grand National Division record books as the winner of the series very first event, at Daytona International Speedway on February 13, 1982. It was the first of his seven career NASCAR Busch Series victories there, including a stretch of five consecutive wins between 1990 and 1994. However, it took him twenty years to win the* *season-opening event for the NASCAR Winston Cup Series. Earnhardt won the Daytona 500 for the first time on February 15, 1998.*

## --------Moving On Up

The biggest factors contributing to the influx of NASCAR Busch Series, Grand National Division drivers coming into the NASCAR Winston Cup Series include the tracks both series race on and the cars with which they race.

The differences between a NASCAR Winston Cup Series and a NASCAR Busch Series race car are in the wheel base, weight, and horsepower tops. While these differences aren't noticeable from the grandstand, they're enough to give a NASCAR Busch Series driver a considerable advantage over drivers from most other racing series when making the move to the NASCAR Winston Cup Series.

And since the NASCAR Busch Series races on a majority of tracks that host NASCAR Winston Cup Series races, the learning curve for a driver making the jump from one series to the other is also lessened.

A third factor to consider is the presence of NASCAR Winston Cup Series drivers in

*Dale Earnhardt won the NASCAR Busch Series inaugural event at Daytona International Speedway on February 13, 1982.*

many NASCAR Busch Series events. A number of the top drivers from NASCAR's number-one series regularly step over to the NASCAR Busch Series level, especially races held in conjunction with the NASCAR Winston Cup Series.

*In addition to his record as the NASCAR Busch Series, Grand National Division's all-time victory leader, NASCAR Winston Cup Series driver Mark Martin also holds the NASCAR Busch Series record for most wins on superspeedways (24, the last at Charlotte Motor Speedway October 4, 1998).*

## --------Why Step Down?

The biggest reason quite a few NASCAR Winston Cup Series drivers are also trying their hand at the NASCAR Busch Series is simple—preparation and money.

Most of the NASCAR Winston Cup Series drivers use their NASCAR Busch Series, Grand National Division programs as an extension of their NASCAR Winston Cup Series efforts, trading information on track conditions and setups, and even using the NASCAR Busch Series races as a test bed for setups that may be used during the next day's race.

*Jack Roush, owner of one of the most successful multicar operations on the NASCAR Winston Cup Series circuit, also holds the NASCAR Busch Series, Grand National Division record for most victories by a car owner in a career. Roush Racing has 31 NASCAR Busch Series victories entering the 1999 season, 26 by Mark Martin and five by Jeff Burton. Burton's*

*last win, at the Miami-Dade Homestead Motorsports Complex in November 1998, broke a tie with Aline Ingram, the wife of two-time champ Jack Ingram, who was the owner of record for thirty of Ingram's 31 career wins.*

## --------But If They Can Race with 'Em . . .

The feeling among the NASCAR Busch Series drivers is that if they can run with, and even beat, the NASCAR Winston Cup Series drivers, it improves their chances

*Jeff Burton is one of many NASCAR Winston Cup Series drivers who can regularly be spotted in a NASCAR Busch Series event.*

*ABOVE: Joe Gibbs Racing drivers Bobby Labonte (left) and Tony Stewart were teammates on select NASCAR Busch Series events in 1998. In 1999, Stewart joined Labonte as a teammate in the NASCAR Winston Cup Series. BELOW: Buckshot Jones also makes the move up to the NASCAR Winston Cup Series in 1999.*

of being picked up by a car owner for a future ride in the top series.

"Just running with those [NASCAR Winston Cup Series] guys can help you learn a lot," said Jason Keller, one of the top drivers in the NASCAR Busch Series the past several seasons.

Already, some of the NASCAR Busch Series "hotshots" are drawing attention from NASCAR Winston Cup Series car owners, and some have a secure future in NASCAR's top division.

At least three drivers who ran a majority of the NASCAR Busch Series, Grand National Division schedule in 1998 are moving to the NASCAR Winston Cup Series ranks in 1999: Roy "Buckshot" Jones, taking his family's Buckshot Racing team up another level; Elliott Sadler, the younger brother of current NASCAR Busch Series star Hermie Sadler, who was signed by the vaunted Wood Brothers Racing team; and Tony Stewart, a former USAC and Indy Racing League open wheel champion who will become a teammate to Bobby Labonte at Joe Gibbs Racing.

There are other hotshots drawing interest from NASCAR Winston Cup Series car owners looking toward the future. Chief among them is Dale Earnhardt Jr., the NASCAR Busch Series, Grand National Division champion in 1998. The youngest son of seven-time NASCAR Winston Cup Series champ Dale Earnhardt won seven races en route to the title, and will return in 1999 to defend it

*Experience in the NASCAR Busch Series in invaluable in many ways. Here, Elliott Sadler gets some advice from NASCAR Winston Cup Series regular Jeff Burton.*

while running a five-race NASCAR Winston Cup Series schedule in preparation for a full-time move in 2000 with his father's Dale Earnhardt Inc. team.

"I'm just so proud of my family and real proud to be involved with my father in racing and be a driver for him," the twenty-three-year-old Earnhardt said. "It's a good relationship we have; it's important to me.

"I'm proud of my father and my grandfather and what they have done. I'm just glad I'm able to be successful at it, too."

Another driver to watch is Matt Kenseth, who finished a close second to Earnhardt in

the '98 NASCAR Busch Series, Grand National Division standings. Kenseth, a native of Cambridge, Wisconsin, gave up a championship-caliber late model ride to move South to join up with former racing foe Robbie Reiser's team in 1997. The move paid off in '98 with three victories and, more important, a five-year "driver development" contract with NASCAR Winston Cup Series car owner Jack Roush, made at the behest of veteran racer Mark Martin.

"Not many people get a job like this," Kenseth said. "It's a great opportunity for me, for sure. I signed a contract with Jack to help them out, and that's been working really well. I never thought an opportunity like this would come along, though, and especially this soon."

Others to keep an eye on in the future include:

**Mike McLaughlin:** This former NASCAR Featherlite Modified Tour and NASCAR Busch North Series star has been solidly impressive since making the move to the NASCAR Busch Series, Grand National Division several years ago, finishing third in the '98 points and fourth in '97.

**Elton Sawyer:** Even though Sawyer is in his late thirties, he's been a mainstay on the NASCAR Busch Series since 1983. Since then he's made 291 starts, with his best finish in the series standings coming in 1998 (fifth). He's also run some NASCAR Winston Cup Series races, with a pole-winning run at North Wilkesboro Speedway.

**Randy LaJoie:** Only the fourth driver to win more than one NASCAR Busch Series, Grand National Division championship. LaJoie suffered through an

*Elton Sawyer and Patty Moise are the only husband and wife to compete against one another on the NASCAR Busch Series.*

After a career on the NASCAR Winston Cup Series, Parsons returned to the NASCAR Busch Series with his own team several years ago.

**Hermie Sadler:** One of two Sadler brothers to run the NASCAR Busch Series, Grand National Division. Sadler won the series rookie-of-the-year title in 1993, and has two career victories to his credit.

**Mike Dillon:** The son-in-law of NASCAR Winston Cup Series car owner Richard Childress. Dillon, thirty-two, moved to the NASCAR Busch Series in 1996 after running up some impressive numbers in late model stock cars. He's even gotten the call from his father-in-law both as a relief driver and a test driver for the NASCAR Winston Cup Series.

off year in 1998 (one win, fourth in points). But he turned heads in the NASCAR Winston Cup Series garage with a solid backup job for injured driver Ricky Craven in his Hendrick Motorsports ride, getting a career-best fifth-place finish in the series at Martinsville Speedway.

**Tim Fedewa:** Another midwestern driver making it big down South. Fedewa has finished solidly in the top ten in the NASCAR Busch Series, Grand National Division point standings four of the past five seasons. He won two races in 1998, pushing his career total to three.

**Phil Parsons:** One of the original members of the NASCAR Busch Series, Grand National Division, Parsons was a series regular when it was formed from the NASCAR Late Model Sportsman Division in 1982.

*Family ties are strong in all NASCAR series. Elliott Sadler left brother Hermie in 1999 as he made the move to the NASCAR Winston Cup Series.*

**Glenn Allen Jr.:** The Ohio native has followed in the footsteps of NASCAR Winston Cup Series star Mark Martin, coming from the American Speed Association to win the NASCAR Busch Series, Grand National Division's rookie-of-the-year award in 1996.

**Mark Green:** The third member of the Owensboro, Kentucky, clan to run in NASCAR's top divisions, the middle of the three Green brothers—his older brother is former NASCAR Busch Series champ David Green, and his younger brother is current NASCAR Busch Series driver Jeff Green. Mark has raced in the NASCAR Busch Series since 1995, and full-time since 1997.

**Jason Keller:** The Greenville, South Carolina, native has been a mainstay on the NASCAR Busch Series, Grand National Division since 1993. Keller made his first NASCAR Busch Series start in 1991, the same year he finished third in the NASCAR Slim Jim All-Pro Series standings while winning four races and leading the series in laps led. Keller has one career NASCAR Busch Series victory, coming at Indianapolis Raceway Park in 1995.

**Jeff Purvis:** The Clarkesville, Tennessee, native is probably one of the toughest superspeedway drivers on the NASCAR Busch Series, Grand National Division, with experience in both the NASCAR Winston Cup Series and Automobile Racing Club of America (ARCA) SuperCar tours. Purvis won eight career ARCA superspeedway events in his career, and has a pair of NASCAR Busch Series victories as well, both coming in 1996 (at Richmond International Raceway and Michigan Speedway).

**Joe Bessey:** The former NASCAR Busch North Series regular made the move South to run the NASCAR Busch Series, Grand National Division full-time in 1993. He has one career NASCAR Busch Series victory to his credit, coming at Dover Downs International Speedway in 1997, and also has an ARCA SuperCar Series victory at Atlanta Motor Speedway in 1996.

**Shane Hall:** A native of Fountain Inn, South Carolina, Shane has raced since his teenage years, winning a World Karting Association (WKA) national championship in 1985 before stepping into stock cars. He has since raced on the NASCAR Slim Jim All-Pro Series, where he led in pole positions in 1993 and won a race in 1994; the NASCAR Busch Series, where he has two career pole positions; and even the NASCAR Winston Cup Series.

**Ed Berrier:** Probably one of the most experienced racers competing on the NASCAR Busch Series, Grand National Division today. Berrier began running the series in 1984, but didn't record his first career NASCAR Busch Series victory until this past season, when he ended a 208-race winless streak at Hickory Motor Speedway. Has also competed on the ARCA SuperCar Series and NASCAR Winston Cup Series.

**Andy Santerre:** Another former NASCAR Busch North Series driver attempting to make it big down South. Santerre won the NASCAR Busch Series, Grand National Division's rookie-of-the-year title in 1998, but didn't begin showing his talent until the second half of the season. Then he won his first pole

*Dave Blaney made the move to the NASCAR Busch Series from the World of Outlaws, where he was a division champion.*

position, at Richmond International Raceway, and had two top-ten finishes, including a career-best fourth at Gateway International Raceway.

***Dave Blaney:*** The former World of Outlaws winged sprint car champion—he won the title in 1995 and was runner-up in

1993, 1994, 1996, and 1997—and moved into the stock-car ranks full-time last season, running most of the NASCAR Busch Series, Grand National Division schedule. In twenty starts, he had three top-ten finishes, and his first career pole position came at Charlotte Motor Speedway.

PART TWO: *Warming Up the Engines*

CHAPTER FOUR

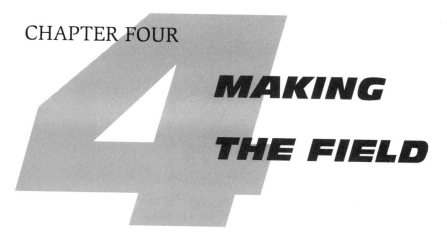

# MAKING
# THE FIELD

**N**ow that you know about some of the history behind the NASCAR Busch Series, Grand National Division and why drivers, both veterans and newcomers, are so attracted to the series, let's move on to the races themselves.

The past several years, NASCAR Busch Series events have drawn more cars and teams than can fit on the track, even at huge venues such as the 2.66-mile Talladega Superspeedway and the 2.5-mile Daytona International Speedway.

To keep things safe and orderly, NASCAR has set limits on how many cars can start a particular race, with the limits based on the size of the track and the number of spaces available on pit road.

That second item is probably the most critical—too few pit stalls or a cramped pit road can make for a difficult situation for the drivers and their pit crews.

On the speedways and some of the short tracks, up to 43 cars will be in the starting lineup for a NASCAR Busch Series, Grand National Division race, while at the "bull-rings"—short tracks usually less than a half mile in length—the field size can range from 33 to 39 cars.

Making the field for a NASCAR Busch Series, Grand National Division race can be quite a chore. Even some top drivers in the NASCAR Winston Cup Series have failed to qualify for NASCAR Busch Series races over the years, testimony to its competitive nature.

Most of the starting lineup is set through time trials, in which each driver entered is given a chance to make one or

*The starting lineup is determined by qualifying, or time trials, with the fastest car starting on the "pole." All starts in the NASCAR Busch Series are double-file.*

two timed laps (depending on the length of the track), with their best time setting their spot.

The order in which the teams qualify is normally based on a blind draw, held the morning of the first round of time trials. A representative from each of the race teams draws a number from a bin under the watchful eyes of a NASCAR official.

While all of the NASCAR Winston Cup Series events have two rounds of time trials, only a handful of NASCAR Busch Series,

Grand National Division events go two rounds. Most set the starting lineup using just one round of qualifying.

*Tommy Ellis holds the NASCAR Busch Series, Grand National Division record for most career pole positions with 28. The driver who is closest to breaking Ellis's record is NASCAR Winston Cup Series driver Mark Martin, who sits third on the NASCAR Busch Series career list with twenty poles. Two-time series champ Sam Ard holds second place with 24 pole wins, but is no longer an active driver.*

Pit road often gets to be a crowded place during a race weekend.

## --------Why Do They Have to Qualify?

The answer to this question is very simple—there's really no other way to set the cars for the race. Actually, qualifying accomplishes several things:

- It groups the cars according to speed, with the faster cars near the front.
- It gives every race team, no matter how poorly it has performed as recently as the previous race, the chance to make things right with a good qualifying run.
- It gives the race fans an additional opportunity to come to the track and see their heroes in action. Although

pole day was once an afterthought, with track promoters opening the gates for anyone who wanted to watch, now hundreds or thousands of fans will turn out at some tracks to watch qualifying sessions.

## --------When Do They Qualify?

When the qualifying trial is held also depends on the track. At facilities that have two rounds of time trials, the first

*Most NASCAR Busch Series events have only one round of qualifying. That makes it even more important for a driver to be prepared and concentrate.*

*The race cars qualify one at a time. A car on the track by itself is clocked by its fastest lap time.*

round is usually held two days before the race, with the second round the following day, while tracks that have just one round of qualifying usually hold it the day before the event.

However, there are exceptions to this, too—for example, The Milwaukee Mile holds both qualifying rounds the day before the race, the first round in the morning and a second round that afternoon, and some of the bullrings like South Boston Speedway and Myrtle Beach Speedway usually have one round of qualifying the day of the race, with the cars that make the show impounded until the race starts.

Whether one round or two, time trials will set only the top thirty-six starters for a particular NASCAR Busch Series, Grand National Division race. The remaining spots in the field are set through the use of provisionals.

Provisionals are starting spots left open for drivers and teams high up in the NASCAR Busch Series point standings, a sort of safety valve in case a driver or team has a bad day at the track. There's also one provisional left open for a past series champion.

In past years some track promoters have also used qualifying races to help fill out the starting lineup. Basically, it's a race, with a certain number of the top finishers moving on to join the starting lineup for the feature race.

One of the last racetracks to use the qualifying race to help set the starting lineup was Charlotte Motor Speedway. Often, those races featured NASCAR Winston Cup Series drivers who struggled in qualifying and were forced into running the qualifying race to even have a chance at making the field. However, 1998 was the final year that speedway officials used the qualifying race, switching to a two-round qualifying setup for 1999 and beyond.

*The order in which a driver qualifies is determined by a blind draw.*

**PIT STOP** *While having to start at the back of the field is a disadvantage, that doesn't mean it's impossible to win a NASCAR Busch Series, Grand National Division race. Chad Little, now a regular on the NASCAR Winston Cup Series, won the 1995 season opener at Daytona International Speedway despite starting 42nd in the 45-car field.*

## --------Your Number's Up

Whether they go one round or two, the qualifying order before each NASCAR Busch Series, Grand National Division race is drawn at random, using a device known to bingo players around the world—a round cage containing numbered balls that is spun to mix them up. Each team sends a representative to draw the team's qualifying position, with the order in which the teams get to draw based on the current car owner points. Beware—miss the drawing for qualifying position, and a NASCAR official will draw for you.

Some race fans may wonder why it's so important in which order the cars qualify,

but there are a number of variables that can make an early or late qualifying run more advantageous. Say you're at Charlotte Motor Speedway and it's a hot, sunny day, but there are clouds on the horizon and they're moving in fast. The track will start out slick, and the first drivers to qualify will have to take it easy. But when the clouds reach the track and cover the sun, the racing surface will cool, providing greater traction. Drivers with later qualifying picks will post better times as a result. Of course, the opposite can happen, too.

Since the temperature generally drops throughout the afternoon, having a later qualifying run is usually preferred. Also, drivers going later in the qualifying session have the advantage of watching their fellow drivers negotiate the track, and therefore have a better idea of what to expect in certain situations.

## --------How Many Laps?

**D**rivers get either one or two laps in which to qualify for a NASCAR Busch Series, Grand National Division race, whether one round or two are held. Why? Generally speaking, drivers get two laps at superspeedways such as Daytona International Speedway or Talladega Superspeedway, where it takes cars longer to reach full speed because of the restrictor plates on their engines. At shorter tracks, however, one lap is usually sufficient for them to reach peak performance.

But the procedure is different at Watkins Glen International, the lone road course on the NASCAR Busch Series circuit. At Watkins Glen, NASCAR officials use a "European qualifying" setup, in which groups of five or six cars are put on the track at one time and given a certain amount of time (usually, five minutes from the time they take the green flag) to make as many laps as they can. The order in which the teams qualify is based on their practice times, with the slowest cars going out first and the fastest making up the final group.

## --------Going for the Pole

**T**he first day of qualifying could set either the first 25 starting positions for the race, or if only one round is used, set the entire starting lineup. At the start of the day, optimism abounds, because any of the four dozen or so cars set to run has a shot at the pole position. In fact, qualifying often brings major surprises, with a rookie, an older vet-

*Being atop the "qualifying board" means you've earned the number one starting spot.*

eran, or an unheralded driver sneaking away with the day's fastest lap.

But most of the time the contenders usually separate themselves from the pretenders in quick order. The cars are held on pit road, then sent onto the track one at a time to run their timed laps. NASCAR uses two methods to keep track of qualifying times. A computer-radio transponder setup, which is also used to score the race, employs small radio transmitters attached to the underside of each race car at a specific spot mandated by officials. As a backup, a timing light system is set up at the start-finish line, in which the clock is started and stopped by the simple act of the race car breaking an infrared light beam shot across the track to a reflector, which in turn bounces the beam back to a receiver.

While it may seem to the casual observer that the cars are all running at the same speed, drivers and their crews, as well as knowledgeable race fans, can listen to a race car's engine and watch the line the driver is running around the track to determine if the car is a contender for the pole. That's a remarkable feat, since the difference between the pole position and the slowest car is usually measured in tenths of a second.

## --------Should I Stay or...?

**N**ASCAR Busch Series, Grand National Division events that have two rounds of qualifying pose an interesting dilemma for the race teams, especially those that were 26th or worse after the first round. They have a tough choice to make—they can "stand on" (keep) their first round time and hope it holds up, or choose to requalify in the second round. The decision is based on several factors, but must be made within five minutes of the end of the final practice before second round qualifying.

One of the major factors taken into account by the race teams is the weather, as well as where the driver was in the standings after the first round of time trials. For example, if a driver qualified 26th on the first day, chances are he's going to make the field. If he qualified 38th, however, he better hit the track the next day for the second round.

There is another factor to be kept in mind: Most racetracks are slower in the second round because of oil and built-up tire rubber on the track. So even if you had a bad time in the first round of qualifying, there's no guarantee that you'll do any better the second day.

Either way you look at it, the drivers and teams face a gamble, because if a driver decides to requalify, his first round time is removed from the books. If he fails to qualify in the second round, even if his first round

time would have put him in the field...too bad, he's going home.

## --------Second Best

**N**o one wants to pick up a dreaded "DNQ," which is racing slang for "Did Not Qualify." That's NASCAR's equivalent of missing out on the big party, sitting at home while the rest of your friends have a good time.

Nothing is more disappointing for a race team—whether in the NASCAR Busch Series, Grand National Division or NASCAR Winston Cup Series—than packing everything back on the hauler and leaving the track the day before the race. So second round qualifying, full of drivers who failed to make the field in the first round, can be a tense affair.

Some simple math underscores the urgency the race teams face: If 49 teams show up to qualify for an event that has a maximum field of 43 starting spots, then at least six teams will have to go home.

The best starting position a second round qualifier can hope for is 26th, as the top 25 spots are locked in by their first-round times. It's not unusual to have one or more second round qualifiers post better times than many of the cars in the top 25. But, more often than not, the second round speeds are slower.

## --------How Can I Get a Provisional?

**S**ometimes even the best drivers and teams have an off day, or even worse, two off days in a row. That's why NASCAR has something known as provisional starting positions, as mentioned above, to make the race. The main reason for provisional starting positions is to provide a spot for regulars and contenders who have had tough luck during the weekend and not made the race by their qualifying speed.

As the number of teams committing to run the full NASCAR Busch Series, Grand National Division season has increased, as well as the number of NASCAR Winston Cup Series drivers who choose to run a limited schedule, NASCAR's provisional system has undergone modifications.

Simply put, there are seven provisional starting positions available for each race. The first four provisional spots—37 through 40—are assigned to teams that are in the top 25 in NASCAR Busch Series, Grand National Division car owner points. The next two–provisional starting positions 41 and 42—go to teams that are outside the top 25 in the NASCAR Busch Series car owner standings.

The final provisional starting position— that's the 43rd starting spot for the race— goes, if needed, to any past NASCAR Busch Series, Grand National Division champion entered in the race who failed to make the field on his qualifying time. If two or more champions are eligible, then the most recent titlist gets the provisional.

One final thing: NASCAR Winston Cup Series drivers are not eligible to use provisional starting positions in the NASCAR Busch Series. Under the NASCAR Busch Series, Grand National Division rules, a driver becomes ineligible to use a provisional if he is in the top 35 in the NASCAR Winston Cup Series point standings, or

has made five or more NASCAR Winston Cup Series starts that season or in the previous year.

## --------Rainy Day Blues

**O**kay, that's all well and good, with qualifying and provisionals and all that. But what happens if Mother Nature decides to intervene and drop a few inches of rain on the racetrack, washing out qualifying? The answer to that depends on the situation.

If qualifying has begun and has to be stopped because of rain or darkness, no matter how many cars have run, then NASCAR normally picks up where qualifying left off, at the earliest possible time. That could be hours later, after the rain stops and the track has been dried, or the next day.

But if the showers don't stop and qualifying has to be cancelled, then a whole new set of rules come into play.

For starters, the top 35 in the NASCAR Busch Series, Grand National Division car owner points get into the race, based on their position in the standings at the time, with the leading team in points getting the pole, the second-place team starting on the outside of the front row, and so on.

Then the defending champion of the NASCAR Busch Series, Grand National Division gets a spot, if he hasn't already qualified for the race by being in the top 35 in NASCAR Busch Series car owner points.

The remaining starting positions for the race will go to drivers who won at least one

*Rain can bring qualifying to an end in a big hurry. Drivers will have to wait until the track is dry, or will start the race by car owners' point standings.*

race during the course of the current or past season, and a car owner whose driver is a past NASCAR Busch Series, Grand National Division champion.

If that has not filled out the starting lineup—remember, up to 43 drivers can start the race—then the remaining starting spots will be filled from the entry blank postmarks of the remaining drivers who have yet to make the field. That's why getting the entry blanks for the race back to NASCAR and the track where the event will be held is a priority for many race teams.

## --------Once the Field Is Set

Once the starting lineup is set, the teams can pick where they want to stop on pit road during their gas-and-tire stops. A drawing is held after the final round of qualifying, in which a team representative (usually the crew chief) makes their selection.

The order of how the teams pick their pit stall is determined on how they qualify, with the pole winner going first, the second-fastest qualifiers going next, and so on until all the pit stalls are selected. This makes qualifying even more critical, because a bad run can leave a team stuck in a bad pit area, even forced to pit on the backstretch of those tracks that have pit roads on both straightaways.

With many cars trying to race in the NASCAR Busch Series, competition during qualifying gets harder each race.

In past years, the selection procedure was somewhat different—the defending NASCAR Busch Series, Grand National Division champion got to make the first choice, no matter how he qualified, followed by the top ten drivers in the current point standings, then followed by the rest of the field, based on their qualifying times.

CHAPTER FIVE

# 5 APPLYING FOR THE JOB

**B**efore a team can even think of entering a NASCAR Busch Series event, their driver must meet certain criteria set down by NASCAR to be eligible to compete.

The basic requirements are simple: You must be at least 16 years of age; but you don't even have to have a valid driver's license.

But wait—not just any sixteen-year-old can walk out of the stands, hop into a car, and compete in a NASCAR Busch Series, Grand National Division race. There are other criteria that must be met.

First of all, remember that driving a 3,300 pound car isn't easy. While the drivers may not have the experience of their counterparts on the NASCAR Winston Cup Series, they have worked their way through the ranks of other forms of racing, such as regional NASCAR touring series.

Something other than pure driving experience enters here. As much as a driver learns

about getting around speedways of various shapes and sizes, he learns just as much about race cars. This is important, because the more a driver knows about how to set up a car, how to get it feeling right on the track, and what to do to make it run better, the more he increases his worth.

Whatever path a driver follows, as a rule a NASCAR Busch Series, Grand National Division driver has spent years honing himself and gaining experience to make the move to NASCAR's No. 2 touring series. His goal is to do well in the NASCAR Busch Series, so he can gain the attention of car owners on the NASCAR Winston Cup Series.

## --------What's the Plan?

**O**kay, you want to drive for a NASCAR Busch Series, Grand National Division team. There are certain steps you have to go through before anyone will let you get behind the wheel of a race car, much less take one on the track.

The first is undergoing a complete physical examination, with a full report submitted to NASCAR before the start of the season. The examination, either conducted by the driver's personal physician or doctors at Daytona International Speedway, includes a drug test.

Next, if a driver is new to the NASCAR Busch Series, Grand National Division, he or she must submit a detailed résumé to NASCAR officials, detailing not only what

*Drivers are quick to announce new sponsors, but not always the amount of money behind the deal.*

racing series they have competed in in past years, but at what racetracks and who they drove for. Those résumés are thoroughly checked out, and any embellishments are quickly flagged.

Some drivers may also have to undergo driving ability tests, in which they would have to run practice laps under the eyes of several NASCAR officials and drivers in order to determine whether or not the wannabe drivers can handle a NASCAR Busch Series race car.

In some instances, preliminary approval may be given, but only for certain racetracks. For example, a driver who spent most of his career running short tracks may be required by NASCAR to run one or two NASCAR Busch Series, Grand National Division short track events, then one or two "intermediate" track events before being allowed to run on the high-speed tracks such as Talladega Superspeedway or Daytona International Speedway.

## --------Don't Show Me the Money

U nlike other professional sports stars, NASCAR Busch Series, Grand National Division teams, sponsors, and drivers seldom reveal the terms of their financial agreements. You hear about multiyear, multi-million-dollar contracts in other sports, but not in NASCAR. That's largely because drivers are considered independent contractors and make their own individual deals with their car owners. While contracts are the norm, some drivers and team owners reach an agreement and seal the deal with a handshake.

In most cases, a driver's compensation is based on three things: a salary, a share of the race winnings, and marketing and licensing opportunities.

The amounts of each vary in each case. Some drivers make more than others, because of their success on the track, their agreement with the team owner and sponsor, and/or their ability to enhance their off-track revenue by taking advantage of on-track success and off-track popularity.

So there is no set minimum—a driver's annual salary is agreed upon between himself and the team owner. While salaries for a NASCAR Busch Series, Grand National Division driver aren't as good as those enjoyed by NASCAR Winston Cup Series drivers, they can reach six figures.

A driver also splits the winnings from each race, as well as any postseason points fund or bonus money, with the team owner. Simply put, the better the team finishes, the more money the driver and car owner get. While the percentage varies from team to team, most NASCAR Busch Series drivers usually get anywhere from ten to forty percent of the winnings and postseason bonuses. That's why the effort to win, or to finish as high as possible, is intense: because there's more money at stake.

Then there are the deals the driver puts together with the sponsors, often negotiating contracts for personal appearances and to perform other services, including marketing the sponsor's products. Again, the dollar amounts of these contracts vary, and not all sponsors offer personal services contracts, but they're becoming more and more common in NASCAR Busch Series, Grand National Division racing.

You also may see a driver, crew chief, or car owner sporting particular items with sponsor logos, stuff like sunglasses, hats, jackets, or shirts. In many cases they have negotiated personal services contracts with that sponsor to promote that particular item or brand.

But probably the fastest-growing part of NASCAR Busch Series, Grand National Division racing is the licensing of drivers' names and likenesses to various souvenir and collectible products, which range from hats and T-shirts to jackets, coolers, books, stationery—you name it, and someone out there is probably making it.

Many drivers work in conjunction with NASCAR, which has a huge licensing and marketing department. However, unlike many other major league sports, in which the league controls most programs, NASCAR drivers control and coordinate their own licensing programs. The drivers earn a percentage—called a "royalty"—of every officially licensed product sold bearing their name or likeness. This percentage varies with the individual deals made.

## ⸺⸺⸺*Okay, I've Been Cleared...*

Okay, you've made it through the approval process, and NASCAR has given you the green flag to go racin' in a NASCAR Busch Series, Grand National Division event.

Slow down a second, though—you can't go on the track just yet.

New drivers are required to sit in on the rookie orientation meeting, usually held the morning before the first practice session begins, in which NASCAR officials discuss the "rules of the road" concerning that particular track. In addition, a veteran driver—normally, this is one of the perks the defending NASCAR Busch Series, Grand National Division champion gets—talks to the rookies about the racing groove and where the trouble spots can be found.

Miss that meeting, rookie, and you get to sit on top of your race team's hauler for the first practice session and watch all the other drivers, missing valuable time on the track in order to get the car set up.

Once practice is over and you've made the race, there's another meeting you'll have to attend, for drivers and crew chiefs,

*There's usually plenty of traffic on the racetrack, so knowing the "rules of the road" are important at any event.*

held the morning of the race (or afternoon, if the race is at night). Normally held at least two hours before the starting time of the event, this meeting gives NASCAR officials one last chance to go over the rules with the drivers, crew chiefs, and spotters, as well as to listen to suggestions on how procedures can be improved.

Miss that meeting, and a driver loses his spot in the qualifying order and has to move to the very back of the field. That would be embarrassing, especially if you were supposed to start on the pole position!

## --------Hey, Let's Go Race!

**N**ow that the driver/crew chief meeting is over with, we can go racing...but there are a few things you'll have to watch out for on the track, as well.

*The checkered flag is the one drivers want to see the most, and first.*

One of the most important things a driver needs to know is the meaning of the colored flags used by NASCAR officials in the flag stand.

Now just about everyone knows what the green flag means (start the race), and the meaning of the checkered flag (the race is over), but what about all the other flags? Here's a brief synopsis of what the other flags mean, and when they're used:

***Blue Flag with Yellow Stripe.*** Also called the passing flag or "move over" flag. It is waved by the flagman to let slower cars know when the leader is catching up to them.

***Yellow Flag.*** Sometimes called the caution flag. This is waved when there's a problem on the track, such as an accident or debris, and NASCAR officials need to slow the field down to take care of the problem.

***Red Flag.*** When this flag is waved, it means the race must be stopped immediately, either because of the weather or serious problems on the track, such as a major accident involving a number of cars.

***Black Flag.*** Waved when NASCAR officials want a driver to report to the pits. Their car number is also displayed on a special board on the flag stand, and a driver has three laps to report to the pits before NASCAR officials stop scoring that driver's laps.

***Black Flag with White Cross.*** Bad news. It means you've not only been black-flagged, but that since you didn't go to pit road within three laps, your scorecard has been pulled and the laps you continue to run aren't being counted.

***White Flag.*** This means the race is almost over. It's waved when there's just one lap to go.

## --------What's Going On?

The NASCAR official in charge of handling the flags is called the "flagman," and he controls the race. On restarts, while the leader can control the pace once the safety car pulls off the track, it is the flagman who actually gives the command to begin racing again.

The flagman and his assistant also handle the black flag and number display board, and serve as a set of eyes for the NASCAR officials in the control tower in case there's something on a race car that needs to be checked out, such as a report of an oil leak or tire rub.

Knowing what the flags mean is important, but so is how to let your fellow drivers know what you plan to do. Normally, this is done with the use of hand signals, and lets the other drivers know whether you're trying to slow down, which way you plan to go, or if you're trying to get someone to team up with you in the draft!

The hand signals are simple—a waving hand means "I'm slowing down," a hand waved in a tomahawk-chop means that the driver wants to hook up in a draft, and pointing to one side of the car or the other lets the driver behind you know which side he should pass on.

Spotters—a team member overlooking the track—can also play a major role here, too. From their perch, they can see when a driver has someone coming up behind or beside him, and can relay messages to another team's spotter for transmission to their driver. That can be vital when two or more drivers decide to hook up in a draft, since at the near–200 mph speeds at tracks like Daytona and Talladega, fractions of a second count.

A future NASCAR Busch Series, Grand National Division driver also needs to know about safety equipment and procedures. Protective fire suits and high-density crash helmets are a MUST before getting in a race car, as well as lap and shoulder belts, neck braces, window nets, and shock-absorbing padding on the roll bars and other exposed surfaces inside the race car.

*Drivers have many devices inside their car in order to protect them during a race.*

CHAPTER SIX

# COME ONE, COME ALL

Members of a NASCAR Busch Series, Grand National Division team may come from all over the country, but they have one thing in common—they love racing and winning.

Being a race team crewman isn't a glamorous job—being on a NASCAR Busch Series team can be hard work, with long hours and extensive travel.

But for those involved, there is nothing more rewarding than helping work on, set up, and service a fast race car, one that's capable of winning races. And when that car actually does win a race, that's usually the time when the crew smiles and admits that all the hard work and long hours were worth it.

## -------How Many Make Up a Team?

These days, most NASCAR Busch Series, Grand National Division teams are housed in spacious shops that have the latest in equipment and tools. But nothing works right without the team members' expertise and skill.

The number of people that work on a team varies, and it really comes down to one thing—the kind of financial resources a team has.

Some of the better-financed teams can and do employ specialists in such areas as chassis and shock absorber setup, or use gear and transmission specialists. But unlike

*A team can consist of many, but only seven members make up the pit crew.*

NASCAR Winston Cup Series teams, however, which do most of their mechanical work—such as building chassis and engines—in-house, most NASCAR Busch Series, Grand National Division teams buy their chassis and have their motors built by an outside supplier.

The person who makes it all work is the crew chief. His job is multidimensional—not only is he responsible for making decisions about the race car and pit strategy, but he's also responsible for the conduct and actions of his race team crew.

On top of that, the crew chief is also part coach, motivating and communicating with his driver and crew, and part mechanic, able to make the decisions on what to change on the race car to improve the handling or what needs to be worked on when there's a problem.

Strategy is a central part of NASCAR Busch Series, Grand National Division competition, and for a crew chief, that means determining when to pit and what to do dur-

ing each pit stop. It also means determining when not to pit. He evaluates the pit crew and decides what exactly will be done on each pit stop and who will do each job.

Further, the crew chief is responsible for the quality of the team, like the coach in any professional sport. He has to motivate, energize, and communicate with the various crew members, and has to help develop the talents of his crew and use the right people in the right jobs. Teamwork is key here, and it is the crew chief's responsibility to see that it exists. If members of a team aren't working well together, then the entire team will suffer. A good coach in any sport gets his team members to function as one, with the team's goals in mind.

It also goes without saying that a crew chief has to know pretty much everything there is to know about a race car, from the engine to the chassis to the suspension. He has to understand fully how a car works and what it takes to make it run at optimum efficiency.

But the crew chief can't do the job alone. He usually has a close relationship with his driver. Few NASCAR Busch Series, Grand National Division teams—heck, few race teams in any series period—have been successful without the right chemistry between the driver and the crew chief. They have to trust each other. A good crew chief will always try to communicate with and accommodate his driver. After all, it's the driver who has to run all those fast miles in the car. If something is not right on the car, the driver must be able to communicate the problem to the crew chief so he can fix it.

The crew chief maintains constant communication with his team and driver during a race.

*The pit crew must be prepared at all times to service their driver's car.*

**PIT STOP** Some crew chiefs go well beyond the call of duty and actually perform pit crew duties, such as changing tires themselves. In fact, being a member of a pit crew and gaining valuable hands-on experience (learning from another crew chief, obviously) is how many crew chiefs are born.

## --------Who Else Makes Up a Race Team?

If you look in the pit areas of any NASCAR Busch Series, Grand National Division team, you'll see a lot of people. That's because it takes a crew to not only work on the car during the week at the track, but to service the car during pit stops and even get the pit area set up before the race begins.

The actual responsibility for the pit stops, though, is handled by the "over-the-wall"

crew. NASCAR limits the number of crewmen that can go over the wall on a pit stop to seven people, but each one has a specialized job where a slight slip or bobble can spell the difference in track position.

The "over-the-wall" crew is composed of:

**The front tire changer:** His job is to change the right- and left-front tires, as well as make any chassis adjustments necessary to the front suspension. More often than not, that involves either the removal of or inserting a spring rubber into the springs in the suspension.

**The rear tire changer:** Similar to the front tire changer, but he handles the right and left rear tires. Like the front changer, he will also be responsible for any chassis adjustments that need to be made.

**Jack man:** Probably the most important crewman on the pit stop. It's his job to jack the car up so the tires can be replaced. The jack man uses a specially designed and engineered jack that is very light (about twenty pounds) but powerful, allowing him to get the car off the ground in just two or three pumps of the handle. When he's done on the right side, he then does the same on the left side. It's then that his job becomes all the more important, because race car drivers have been trained that when the jack drops, they GO! Drop the jack before all the lug nuts are tightened, and it means a bad stop, a race car returning to pit road, and maybe even a wreck when the wheels fall off the car.

**Gas man:** Responsible for fueling the race car. He uses a special gas can (it holds eleven gallons, and two of these cans are used on each pit stop) equipped with a valve that fits into the race car's gas

*The hurried pace of a pit stop must be performed without mistake.*

port and empties the fuel quickly. The gas man must be extremely strong, for a full can can weigh upwards of ninety pounds.

***The gas catch man:*** He is responsible for catching any overflow of fuel. He uses a special container that attaches to the race car's gasoline overflow vent, allowing him to gather up gas that overflows from a full tank. The amount of gas caught in the catch can is sometimes critical to a team's race strategy, because it can give the team a rough calculation of just how much fuel is in the fuel cell. He may also be responsible for holding the gas can in place while the gas man gets a second full can.

***Tire carriers:*** There are usually two tire carriers, one each for the front and

rear. They bring the tire changers the replacement tires and help guide them onto the lug nuts so they can be tightened properly. The rear tire carrier may also be responsible for making chassis adjustments using a wrench on the jack bolts in the rear suspension, either taking out or putting in a round of wedge to improve the car's handling.

There are also other crewmen—often referred to as "utility crewmen"—who handle such tasks as giving the driver water during pit stops, washing the windshield of a race car, holding the pit stop sign, cleaning

the front grill of debris, or even setting up and packing up the pit equipment before and after the race.

All the members of a race team are important to the success of the team. The driver can't work on the car by himself, the crew chief can't decide what changes need to be made to the car without feedback from the driver, and the crew can't get to victory lane without giving the driver a good car and good pit stops.

## --------*Back at the Shop...*

**U**nlike many NASCAR Winston Cup Series teams, which have scores of crewmen who remain at the race shop work-

*The gas man and catch-can man play an important role during a pit stop. Many races have been won and lost on fuel mileage.*

ing on the cars that will be used at the next race, many NASCAR Busch Series, Grand National Division crew members pull "double duty"—not only do they work on the cars at the shop, but they travel to the races and even go over the wall to do pit stops.

Most race teams employ the following specialists:

*Fabricators:* In essence, the fabricator builds the race car. Specifically, he takes the sheet metal delivered from the car manufacturers and attaches it to the frame of the car. He also shapes and hangs custom-formed pieces of sheet metal,

*A pit crew can do a four-tire change and fill the car with gas in fewer than 20 seconds.*

most of which he's fashioned himself. And after all that is done, it must conform to several sets of NASCAR body templates.

***Chassis specialist:*** While the fabricator works on the outside of the race car, the chassis specialist is responsible for much of the internal workings. This person works with shock absorbers, springs, sway bars, weigh ratios—to keep it simple, he's responsible for the overall handling of the race car while it's on the track.

***Mechanics:*** Most NASCAR Busch Series, Grand National Division teams have several mechanics, especially those who can handle many jobs, such as working on the brakes one minute, welding part of the chassis together the next, shaping the body another time, painting the car another moment, or machining parts and pieces for the car at other times.

***Truck driver:*** This is the first person to leave the shop for the racetrack, and usually the last person to get back after a race. He's responsible for the team's 18-wheel tractor-trailer rig, which hauls two race cars (the primary and a backup), pit and mechanical equipment, and spare engines and parts to keep a race team going for a hard weekend at the track. He also has to keep it properly serviced, stocked with all the necessary equipment and supplies (from spare parts to food), as well as keep it cleaned.

***Team manager:*** He (or she) is responsible for the overall operation of the race team, which means handling most, if not all, of the administrative and personnel work. The managers pay the bills, set the schedules, hire workers, do just about everything that needs to be done to keep a race team running smoothly day in and day out.

*Of course, like any good business, a NASCAR Busch Series, Grand National Division race team has all of the necessary "nonracing" personnel, including marketing and public relations representatives, receptionists, secretaries, accountants, office managers, and even folks who sweep the floors.*

# CHAPTER SEVEN

# 7 PIT STOPS

**W**hile the driver can make a difference on the track during a NASCAR Busch Series, Grand National Division race, races are more often won or lost in the pits, with a second gained or lost on pit road the difference between winning and losing.

Conversely, good or bad pit strategy can spell the difference between putting on a late run to the front, or seeing a driver flounder on the track in the closing laps as the tires on his race car wear out.

## ----High Stakes Poker

**A**ll that responsibility falls on the shoulders of the crew chief, but he faces a different set of challenges and restrictions than his counterparts on the NASCAR Winston Cup Series do.

*Keeping track of fuel mileage, tire usage, and different setups are important during a race weekend.*

"It's like playing poker—you've got to know when to hang onto your cards, and when to let 'em go," said Donnie Richeson, who has been a crew chief for both NASCAR Busch Series, Grand National Division and NASCAR Winston Cup Series teams. "It's a different ball game altogether, really. There's a lot of similarities, but you also have to think a lot differently with a Busch car than you would with a Cup car."

For starters, NASCAR Busch Series, Grand National Division races are shorter than NASCAR Winston Cup Series events. For example, the NASCAR Busch Series race at Charlotte Motor Speedway is only 300 miles (200 laps), while the NASCAR Winston Cup Series events are 500 and 600 miles (334 and 400 laps, respectively).

## ·······*Tires Are the Thing*

**B**ecause of the difference in race length, fuel mileage sometimes plays a factor in determining pit strategy, but there's one factor unique to the NASCAR Busch Series, Grand National Division that plays the biggest role.

It's called the "tire rule," regulations instituted by NASCAR to keep costs down by limiting the number of sets of tires NASCAR Busch Series teams can change during a caution flag.

The teams can change as many sets of tires as they like when the race is running

*NASCAR instituted a "tire rule" which helps keeps a team's costs down. The rule limits the number of tires a team can change during a caution flag.*

under the green flag, but no race team wants to do that—it means lost positions and lost laps on the track, positions and laps that may never be made up.

So for a crew chief, figuring pit strategy has been likened to a high-stakes gamble, only there's no chips on the table, just a race team that can win or lose.

"The tire situation is the whole key to it," Richeson said. "In NASCAR Winston Cup races, you kinda figure things backward. You know how far you can go on gas, but you have to wonder if the tires will last that long. If they can, then you can kinda dictate how you'll do your stops, like 'I wanna be pitted by this lap....'

"But in a NASCAR Busch Series, Grand National Division race, the first caution flag may dictate whether you can make it all the way on gas and can finish the race on just one stop. Or if you can't, then you've got to make a decision on how you're gonna divide the second half of the race up, and how long you hang on before stopping."

The NASCAR Busch Series, Grand National Division teams actually begin looking at tire wear during practice in the days before the race. Each team entered in the race gets three sets of Goodyear tires to use for practice and qualifying, and no more unless they run in the second round of time trials, in which case a fourth set of tires are issued.

*The penalty for violating the "tire rules" are severe—a one-lap penalty per extra tire changed during a yellow flag. However, exceptions are made to the rule for tires that have gone flat or have been damaged because of an on-track accident.*

## --------Caution, Caution, When Are the Cautions?

**M**ost teams prefer making their pit stops during caution flags. Not only does it give the crew a better chance of making a stop without a mistake hurting them, but it gives them a chance to work on the handling of the race car to make it better.

However, more and more races are being decided on fuel mileage, especially on the superspeedways like Michigan Speedway and the California Speedway, a pair of two-mile ovals that are considered some of the easiest tracks to race on in the NASCAR Busch Series, Grand National Division.

"You can never depend on a caution," Richeson said. "Today's races are becoming more and more green-flag finishes. Mechanically, the cars are a lot better and the engines are definitely more reliable than they've ever been. That means we're seeing fewer and fewer cautions. When you see a caution now, it's usually because of an accident and not because of a mechanical failure."

## --------Time to Gas It Up

**T**he fuel cell of a NASCAR Busch Series, Grand National Division racer hold 22 gallons of high-octane 76 racing gasoline, but the number of laps a car can run on one tank depends on a number of factors. The size of the track, how a car is set up, how long one car drafts (running nose-to-tail) with another one, even how the driver is handling his race car, can all affect the fuel mileage.

With no fuel gauge in the car to tell a driver how much fuel he has left, he depends on measurements taken by his crew during practice and the race to tell him how far he can go before having to stop. The only thing that can tell a driver when he's got a problem with fuel is a fuel-pressure gauge, which drops when the tank begins running out, and the sound of his race car's motor, which will sputter and die when it's starved of fuel.

Just imagine a driver leading a race, only to run out of gas just past the entrance of pit road on a track like the 2.66-mile Talladega Superspeedway. That would force the driver to coast all the way around the track without power, and knock him from leading the race to going several laps down.

Teams attempt to prevent that from happening by monitoring the weight of the fuel cans used to fill the car with gasoline. They weigh the cans when they're full and again when they're empty, then once again right after a pit stop with what fuel remains in the gas can and catch can. These numbers are used to calculate the fuel mileage their race car is getting, which can then be used to determine the number of laps their car can run before having to pit again.

## --------*Where Are We Running?*

**A**nother factor that comes into play when making decisions on whether or not to pit is just where your car is running on the track, and how far back it would put your driver if he stopped.

*Each can of gas holds 22 gallons of 76 racing fuel. A team uses the amount of fuel left in the can after a pit stop to help determine fuel mileage.*

"Track position is a big factor," Richeson said. "You've got to be constantly thinking about where you are on the track. It's not as bad on the NASCAR Winston Cup Series, because you're gonna have seven or eight pit stops during the day, you may choose to spend some time in the pits and really adjust your car. That'll slow your stop down, but you can choose to do that the first few stops so you can get geared up for the rest of the race.

"But in a NASCAR Busch Series, Grand National Division race, you've only got one or two chances, period. You better hit it right coming right off the truck, because you don't get the chances to adjust on the car. There's just not enough laps to come back. It's a whole different scenario."

## ⸺⸺Gotta Stop . . . What Do We Do?

Okay, you've got to make a pit stop— so what's the call, crew chief? Two tires or four?

Most pit stops during caution flags (and even some green-flag stops) are four-tire stops, taking fuel out of the equation. It takes longer to change four tires on a race car than it does to dump a pair of eleven-gallon cans of gas into the fuel cell, so a driver can be assured of having a full tank when he pulls back on the track.

It's in the closing stages of the race, where time or lack of it, becomes a factor.

If the crew has calculated that their driver can go 55 laps on a tank of fuel and there are 57 laps to go, most crew chiefs and drivers would say, depending on where they're running on the track, that staying out is worth the gamble. Most drivers and crew chiefs would rather go for the win than settle for anything else. After all, what's the difference between finishing second and 22nd?

A lot, because track position also means much-needed points towards the NASCAR Busch Series, Grand National Division championship. A twenty-position swing is worth 73 points, and that's a big difference in the points race.

At the end, it really comes down to what the leader of the race does. When the leader makes his move, anything planned by the other teams can be altered, or thrown out the window.

Ultimately, a team's pit strategy is often based on how and where their driver is running on the track. It doesn't matter how many times a driver has come down the frontstretch battling for the win, or even if it's his first time running for the checkered flag—every situation is different, with a different track and different cars.

The only sure thing is that all drivers know they can't win the race just by leading the first lap. After that, it's just a game of high-stakes poker.

CHAPTER EIGHT

# 8 *INSPECTED BY NASCAR*

atching over the teams in the NASCAR Busch Series, Grand National Division garage area at every race is a squad of inspectors, looking and checking to make sure that each of the cars stay within the rules. At every event there are at least three dozen officials, with half of those involved in the actual inspection process. Inspection is probably the most important and crucial part of race weekend, because as the weekend progresses, the teams constantly make changes to their race cars.

"We can't ever quit trying to provide a level playing field for all of the teams," said NASCAR Busch Series, Grand National Division director John Darby. "Yet at the same time, the teams can never quit seeking advantages over their fellow competitors.

"It's not a war, it's not us-versus-them, it's all of us working together to achieve a common goal. If you're a competitor, the one thing you don't have to worry about is that the team next to you is doing something you wanted to do but didn't because of a rule. That's our big job—to instill that confidence among all the teams."

## ⸺⸺⸺Where Do the Officials Come From?

wo of the questions race fans ask most often are: "How can I get a job with NASCAR?" and "How can I become a NASCAR official?"

Becoming a NASCAR Busch Series, Grand National Division official often begins the same way it does for many drivers: in another NASCAR touring series or other racing circuits. Getting involved in racing at the grass-roots level is one of the best ways to

*The NASCAR Busch Series has many NASCAR officials who keep a close eye on every team during the weekend.*

learn many aspects of the sport, from competition to inspection to flagging races to even running the public address system. This can provide invaluable experience that could take you up the ranks to one of NASCAR's national touring series.

Other NASCAR officials have gained experience through mechanical backgrounds. It would be impossible to list all of the areas from which every official comes, but the first requirement NASCAR looks for, no matter what your background may be, is the willingness to work hard.

# --------What Do They Do?

**B**efore any cars can roll onto the track, they are required to be inspected by NASCAR officials, who look over every aspect of each race car entered in the event. That ranges from the engine to the roll bars to the front and rear spoilers, the fuel cell, and just about anything else you can imagine.

"Sometimes they use rulers, sometimes they use templates, and sometimes we use fine measurement tools like micometers," NASCAR director John Darby said. "Everything that's being looked at, inspected, or checked is all just to make sure that it's within the measurements and shapes defined in the rule book."

The main part of the process is the inspection line, during which the body style, roof height, and overall car weight of every NASCAR Busch Series, Grand National Division race car is checked.

More than a dozen templates, cut to conform to the approved body style measurements of Fords, Chevrolets, and Pontiacs, are applied to different areas of the car—the rear quarter panels, the deck lid, roof line, doors, everything—so NASCAR officials can make sure the body of each car meets the standard design approved by NASCAR.

Another measuring device is also used to check the bodies—the inspector's experienced eye. While a race car may fit all the templates, there are still areas that aren't covered by them, areas NASCAR officials don't like to see being monkeyed around with too much.

"The templates are probably one of our major guidelines," Darby said. "But it's conceivable that you can build a car that would fit every template and doesn't look a thing like the car should be. Obviously, our templates don't encompass every single square inch of the car. While we constantly try to remove the eyesight inspection, there is an overall appearance that's laid out in the rule book that we use as a guideline.

"Even though we have many, many, many templates and we strive to keep that showroom stock appearance to the best of our ability, there's enough differences between a stock vehicle that sometimes adjustments and things are modified to adjust for that."

*Using templates is one way that NASCAR officials inspect the race cars.*

Then the height of the race car, from the ground to the roof, is checked, as is the overall weight, ground clearance of the front air dam, the height and width of the rear spoiler, the size of the fuel cell, and the frames and roll bars, which have to be the proper thickness.

Last but not least, the engines are "whistled" to check the compression ratio, which in a NASCAR Busch Series, Grand National Division motor is a maximum of 9.5-to-1, and the overall cubic inches (limited to 358 ci, just like a NASCAR Winston Cup Series car engine).

All that before the cars even get on the track for practice.

## ---------How Many Inspections?

The inspection process begins anew before the first round of time trials, with every car planning on turning a qualifying lap required to go back through the line again. The top five qualifiers must go through

*Often NASCAR officials will discuss a problem or rule infraction with one another in order to determine the best possible means of action.*

a minimum check—just height and weight—before their positions are official.

Say a car doesn't make the field in the first round of time trials, and the team wants to try again during the second round: Do they have to go back through the inspection line again?

Yep. There's no avoiding it if they want to requalify, and if they're one of the two fastest cars during the second round, they go back through the line again just to have the height and weight checked.

The NASCAR inspectors' job doesn't end there, however.

Every team that made the race must go through the inspection process one more time before they're allowed to push their cars onto pit road so they can be lined up on the starting grid.

## ---------And During the Race?

The NASCAR officials' jobs reach their peak with the running of the race itself, with almost everything that has taken place in the garage area the past several days moving to pit road.

There is normally one NASCAR Busch Series, Grand National Division official for every two pit stalls on pit road, where he is responsible for monitoring pit stops and enforcing the many rules that govern proper procedure in performing these stops. Like referees in football and basketball, the officials know what to look for and where to look for it.

Not that they merely wait for pit stops to occur. The officials also relay pertinent infor-

mation from the control tower to the crew chiefs regarding the cars for which they're responsible. The control tower watches for problems such as a smoking car, going slower than the minimum required speed, lining up on restarts, and so on. Pit road officials then communicate these issues to the respective crew chief.

The NASCAR officials in the control tower make the decisions regarding the on-track aspects of the race: when to throw a caution, when to dispatch utility trucks, when to start the race. Practically every decision regarding the race is made from the control tower.

But, as with nearly everything else in NASCAR, one person is not responsible for making final decisions. It takes a team of

*One NASCAR Busch Series official can be found for every two pit stalls on pit road. There, they monitor the action during a pit stop very closely.*

several people to make important decisions, often in a matter of seconds.

There are also two NASCAR officials in the flag stand at every NASCAR Busch Series, Grand National Division race. Ironically, the "official starter" seldom gets to start the race; rather, that privilege usually goes to an "honorary starter" named by each NASCAR Busch Series track. From the flag stand, by messages relayed by two-way radio, the flagman and his assistant communicate with drivers with eight flags that have different meanings.

*An official can also be found at the end of pit road. His job is to tell the drivers when they can and cannot return to the racetrack.*

## ——————Scoring the Race

Once the race finally begins, probably the hardest-working NASCAR officials are the ones involved in scoring the event. NASCAR uses four methods of scoring each NASCAR Busch Series, Grand National Division race: transponders, electronic button, manual scoring, and scoring tape.

Transponders are small boxes, smaller than a deck of playing cards, that are mounted under the car near the rear bumper. They transmit a signal to the scoring stand and a series of computers every time the car crosses a line of antennas embedded in the racetrack at the start-finish line.

The second method of scoring, the electronic "button" system, is activated by a scorer provided by each team every time their car crosses the scoring line. That's right—the scorer presses a button every single time their car crosses the line.

At the same time, the scorer makes note of the time on a special display mounted at the scoring line, and writes that time down on a card issued by NASCAR's scoring officials before the start of the race. That's the third scoring method.

The fourth and final method, if needed, is to review a scoring tape that records all information inputted and that runs from the green flag until every car takes the checkered flag to end the race.

## --------*And After the Race Is Over?*

What about after the race? The inspectors' jobs get tougher. The top five finishers, plus one or two others chosen at random, go back through the inspection line for another height-and-weight check.

But the worst is saved for the winner's car, and a few others during the weekend. NASCAR officials tear the engine of the winner's car down completely, as well as the motors of the runner-up, the pole winner, the fastest driver in second-round qualifying, and one other chosen at random.

As part of the tear-down, the cubic-inch displacement and compression ratio are checked again, using more precise measuring devices, and the cylinder heads, intake manifold, and carburetor are all given a good once-over by NASCAR inspectors.

## --------*Uh-Oh . . . They Found Something*

But what happens if NASCAR officials find something that's not quite kosher during their inspection process? Then things get a little more complicated, and it gets kicked upstairs to higher-level officials.

Normally, if something is found wrong during the initial inspection, the penalty is simple—confiscate the part in question and make the team fix the problem and go back

*If an illegal part is found during inspection before the race, NASCAR officials will confiscate the part and the team will have to repair the problem.*

through inspection before being allowed on the track.

But if something is found during post-qualifying inspection, the penalties get a little harsher—in most cases, not only is the offending part or piece confiscated, but the driver's qualifying time is disallowed, forcing him to either requalify during the second round or use a provisional starting berth. Either way, that team is gonna be back in the pack when the green flag falls.

Things get even worse if something is found during the postrace tear-downs. That's when the harshest penalties—fines, suspensions, deduction of points, even taking the win away—can come into play.

Determining such a penalty isn't made by one person, it's the decision of a committee of top-level NASCAR officials. Series Director John Darby, Director of Operations Kevin Triplett, and Senior Vice-President Mike Helton will meet together and with the driver, crew chief, and car owner of the offending team.

*An overall inspection of a race car includes the car's chassis all the way to the fuel cell.*

caught by all the prerace inspections.

"If that happens, then it falls into the laps of our supervisory officials, putting their heads together to see if it was actually a competitive advantage or not. Once that's determined, then penalties are assessed in relationship to the severity of the infraction."

But don't go thinking that what one team got for a penalty will apply across the board. Even though precedents are a major consideration when NASCAR's top officials hand down penalties, each case is also ruled on its own merits.

"Carbon-copy, duplicate situations just seem like they never occur," Darby said. "It's always going to be something new. That's part of the evolution of the sport, the ongoing ingeniousness of the teams working to be better than their competitors. That's one of the things that makes it so neat to be involved in this."

"That's an ongoing battle for us," Darby said. "Every weekend, all the officials strive to do their absolute best not to miss anything. But there are rare occasions, especially when we have to deal with a large volume of cars and the time constraints that go with it, that something might slip by that doesn't get

PART THREE: *The Green Flag*

CHAPTER NINE

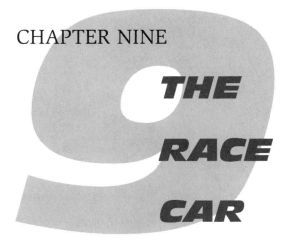

# THE RACE CAR

NASCAR racing began in the 1940s, when the car you drove on the street was the same car you raced on the weekend. What was then known as the strictly stock division has since been named the NASCAR Winston Cup Series. The philosophy of racing a "stock" car held true in NASCAR for many years, and automobile manufacturers took advantage of it. A popular slogan of the time was "Win on Sunday, sell on Monday."

That old philosophy can still be found in NASCAR racing today. Although you can't drive the family minivan in a race at your local speedway, race cars do resemble their street versions. The cars found on a NASCAR Busch Series track are the same style of car you can buy at your local dealer—minus the safety harness and roll bars, of course.

The approved body styles for the NASCAR Busch Series, Grand National Division are the Chevrolet Monte Carlo, the Ford Taurus, and the Pontiac Grand Prix. However, if you take a closer look inside the car and under the hood, you'll quickly spot the differences between the race car version and showroom version.

## --------Stock Car vs. Showroom Car

Beyond the similar body styles, the differences found between the two cars are both noticeable and necessary. Your family car contains such amenities as seat belts, air bags, cushioned seats, heat and air conditioning, and even a stereo for your listening enjoyment. Now look inside a NASCAR Busch Series race car. No cushioned seats. No air conditioning. Not even a stereo!

The race car is built in an effort to provide maximum safety for the driver, not luxury.

The roll cage, safety seat and harnesses, and the detachable steering wheel protect the driver in case of an accident. The air conditioning? Replaced by a cool suit. The stereo? Replaced by a two-way radio that keeps the driver in constant contact with his crew chief and spotter.

In an effort to keep both cars as similar as possible, NASCAR mandates that certain parts remain stock. Those parts include the hood, grill, rear deck lid, and the bumper panels. All of these aspects of a NASCAR Busch Series car are identical to that make's street version.

But if you take a closer look you'll realize that a NASCAR Busch Series car contains a few extra elements:

- **Cowl:** This is a special air duct that routes clean, fresh air directly to the air filter, allowing better combustion.
- **Fuel cell:** The special fuel cell on a race car also includes a "bladder,"

*NASCAR Busch Series race cars look very similar to their street car counterparts in the shape of their body, but hold many differences under the sheet metal.*

which minimizes the risk of fuel spills in case of an accident.

- **Coil springs:** Stiffer coil springs allow the driver to have better control and a better "feel" of the track.
- **Roll cage:** A safety element that helps protect the driver if a problem occurs.
- **Air dam and rear spoiler:** Although found on many sports cars as well, both are functional only on the race car.
- **Brake cooling ducts:** In order to prevent overheating, the brake cooling ducts channel air to the brake rotors.

These differences are only a few, though. Every effort possible is met to create a race car that both performs and protects at the maximum level.

## --------It's Not Your Father's Chevrolet ... or Ford ... or Pontiac

Most race fans see no difference in appearance between a NASCAR Busch Series, Grand National Division race car and those used on the NASCAR Winston Cup Series. In fact, there isn't.

The cars in both series look alike and have a lot of similarities. They're both based on American-made full-size passenger cars, and they have to somewhat resemble the cars we drive on the streets.

Both the NASCAR Busch Series and NASCAR Winston Cup Series also have what is known as the "three-year rule." Basically, it means that no body style can be more than three model years old. For example, 1996 body styles, which were still legal to use in 1998, are no longer approved for the 1999 season.

But there are some differences in the approved body styles between the two series. While the NASCAR Busch Series, Grand National Division and the NASCAR Winston Cup Series both share approval of the Chevrolet Monte Carlo, Pontiac Grand Prix, and Ford Taurus and Thunderbird (1997 model year only), the NASCAR Busch Series also allows the 1997 body styles of the Buick Regal, Mercury Cougar, and Oldsmobile Cutlass Supreme. (The Buick Regal and Oldsmobile Cutlass, however, aren't used on the NASCAR Busch Series, Grand National Division circuit because their manufacturers aren't as heavily involved in NASCAR Busch Series racing anymore.)

## --------Is Anything "Stock" about Stock Cars?

But what is really stock about these "stock cars"? Not much, really—the hoods, roof panel, and trunk lids come from the automobile manufacturers, and the floorboards are stamped from an original mold and provided by suppliers. The rear bumper and front nosepiece can come from either the manufacturer or an aftermarket supplier (someone who builds these parts similar to those built in the factory).

The rest of the car, mainly all the sheet metal that makes up the fenders and quarter panels, is hand-made and shaped by the race team fabricators, then installed at the shop when the race car is built.

The rule books for both series do say, however, that "cars must remain stock in appearance," meaning a Chevrolet Monte Carlo must look like one and not some custom street rod. NASCAR doesn't allow much modification to the body panels, either, except for what is approved to match the templates, and some flaring of the fender wells to get those wide Goodyear racing slicks under the fenders and onto the wheels.

Windshields must also be stock, with the material much like that used on the windshields of regular passenger cars. However, NASCAR does allow the teams, both on the NASCAR Busch Series and the NASCAR Winston Cup Series, to install a one-eighth-inch-thick polycarbonate (plastic, often called Lexan) windshield under the stock windshield, for added protection.

The rear window can be plastic, though, and in both series a full one-piece window

*The front air dam on a NASCAR Busch Series car must have a clearance of four inches.*

has to be in place on the car's right (passenger) side on tracks that are 1.5 miles or longer. The aim is to keep air at high speeds from rushing through the car and making it unstable to the point where it would not stay grounded, especially in a sideways spin. Otherwise, door windows aren't permitted, but a nylon mesh window screen must be installed on the left-side (driver's side) door opening.

## --------*There Are Differences*

**B**ut if you look closer—emphasis on *closer*—there are worlds of differences between the two types of race cars.

For starters, a NASCAR Busch Series, Grand National Division race car is actually

five inches shorter in the wheelbase, the distance from the front wheel's spindle to the rear axle. NASCAR Busch Series cars have a wheelbase of 105 inches, compared to 110 inches for a NASCAR Winston Cup Series racer.

The tread width—the distance across the bottom of the car, measured from the outside of the tire tread on one side to the outside of the tire tread on the other side—is also different. The NASCAR Busch Series cars are allowed a maximum tread width of 60 inches, while the NASCAR Winston Cup Series cars have a little more freedom, varying from 60.25 inches to 60.5 inches.

The weight difference between the cars on both series is also different, though not as much as in past years. NASCAR Busch Series, Grand National Division cars must weigh at least 3,300 pounds, while NASCAR Winston Cup Series cars must weigh in at 3,400 pounds.

There are differences between the front air dams and rear spoilers too. While the NASCAR Winston Cup Series has played with its spoiler and air dam dimensions over the years, looking to achieve parity between Fords, Chevrolets, and Pontiacs, the NASCAR Busch Series has left that alone, requiring a rear spoiler 57 inches wide and 6.5 inches high, and a front air dam clearance of four inches.

Now, what the teams on both the NASCAR Busch Series and NASCAR Winston Cup Series can do with their race cars as far as paint schemes and decaling are almost limitless, except for the car numbers on the door panels and roof. The design and coloring of these must be clear to timing and scoring officials, since the backup systems used by NASCAR to score races is a manually operated "button" hooked to a computer, which registers a lap every time the button is pressed. The scorer pressing the button must be able to easily identify and read the number.

## --------More Differences

There are major differences between a NASCAR Busch Series, Grand National Division racer and a regular passenger car.

The most obvious is in the passenger compartment, which has just one specially designed racing seat, molded to the shape of the driver's body, along with a five-point restraint harness.

There's no air conditioner, although many drivers have a "cool helmet" system installed which blows fresh air over dry ice to cool it down, then pumps it to the driver's helmet to keep his temperature down during the race—a needed device, considering that the passenger compartment of a race car can reach 150 degrees or more during a race.

Of course, there's no AM/FM/CD/cassette multimegawatt stereo system, only a two-way radio so the driver can talk and listen to his spotter, crew chief, and the rest of the crew.

There are no turn signals, headlights, brake lights, or windshield wipers, and just a few dials and switches on a painted metal dashboard. The biggest dial is taken up by the tachometer, but there's no speedometer. There are also gauges for oil and water temperature, oil pressure and fuel pressure.

*Many areas on the car have required minimum and maximum parameters. They include the wheel base, spoiler height, air dam, and weight and height of the car.*

There's a special fuel cell that includes a fuel bladder and safety padding, to cut down the risk of fuel spills during accidents, and there are yards and yards of roll bars and padding to help protect the driver.

There are also "roof flaps," an aerodynamic safety device mandated by NASCAR in 1996. The flaps deploy when a race car gets sideways at high speeds, helping to disrupt the airflow over the car to help keep it grounded.

CHAPTER TEN

# UNDER THE HOOD

While the exterior of a NASCAR Busch Series, Grand National Division racer looks similar to its showroom stock cousin, it's a different story under the hood and in the suspension.

While most passenger cars traveling the highways today sport fuel-injected, computer-controlled four-, six-, or eight-cylinder engines, NASCAR's power plants hark back to the old days of Detroit iron, sporting fire-breathing, carburetor-fed, push-rod V8 engines.

While most passenger cars today glide along the roads in relative comfort, thanks to computer-controlled suspension systems, antilock braking, and automatic transmissions, NASCAR stock cars use power-assisted steering to help guide the brutes, manual transmissions to put the power from the high-revving engine to the ground, and coil springs and gas-filled shock absorbers to keep all four wheels on the ground.

## --------The Heart of the Car

The heart of a NASCAR Busch Series, Grand National Division race car is its engine, an eight-cylinder monster that can pump out nearly 550 horsepower at 8,000 revolutions per minute.

Say what you will about the importance of a car's setup, tires, spoilers, or anything else, but the engine is the key ingredient. If a car isn't handling right on the track, it's a problem that can be solved on pit road, or if some sheet metal gets bent in, it's a simple job to tape it down and put the car back on the track. But develop engine trouble, and quick fixes fall by the wayside. No piece of tape can fix a broken camshaft or valve spring.

Drivers always talk about their engine program and how vital it is to their team's success (or the lack of it), while little men-

*The engine of a race car is often referred to as the heart of the car. A NASCAR Busch Series race car's engine can pump out nearly 550 horsepower.*

tion is ever made of a spring or spoiler program. The importance of a NASCAR Busch Series, Grand National Division race team's engine program is demonstrated by the number of engines each team brings to the racetrack each week.

## --------*Stock vs. Production*

Comparing a passenger car engine to a NASCAR Busch Series, Grand National Division motor is like comparing a rowboat to a high-performance racing boat. They both do the same thing, but one is a lot more efficient...not to mention a heck of a lot faster.

NASCAR goes into detail as to what is and isn't allowed in regard to the engines for both the NASCAR Busch Series and the NASCAR Winston Cup Series, in keeping

with their goal to make the cars of both series as "stock" as possible.

Along those lines, many of the engine specifications must be identical with a factory-produced engine, including the number and angle of cylinders, the location of the camshaft, the number of intake and exhaust valves and ports per cylinder, and the location of the spark plugs. NASCAR also mandates that major components such as the engine block and cylinder heads be produced by the manufacturer for sale to the general public.

However, there are some important differences, as engine builders for both NASCAR Busch Series, Grand National Division and NASCAR Winston Cup Series teams use high-performance parts designed to generate and hold up under high rpm while enduring tough race conditions.

There's a difference, too, between the two series. Though NASCAR engines use carburetors instead of the fuel-injection systems prevalent today in modern-production car engines, Winston Cup Series teams use a single, four-barrel carburetor rated at 830 cfm (cubic feet per minute) and are limited to having a compression ratio of 12 to 1. NASCAR Busch Series racers use engines with a four-barrel carb pumping 390 cfm, and the engine itself is limited to a compression ratio of 9.5 to 1.

The end result? The NASCAR Winston Cup Series engines are more powerful, pumping out more than 720 horsepower, while the

*Even fine tunings on the carburetor could be necessary during the course of a race.*

NASCAR Busch Series, Grand National Division motors top out at 550 horsepower.

The most a passenger car's engine can produce? About 200 horsepower, although some high-performance passenger cars like the Chevrolet Corvette or the Ford Mustang have motors that reach 300 horsepower or more.

*In case you're wondering, NASCAR Busch Series, Grand National Division race cars can get five or six miles* per gallon from their V8 engines, and slightly more than that at the restrictor-plate tracks, Daytona International Speedway and Talladega Superspeedway. With a 22-gallon gas tank, it's no wonder pit stops are such an important part of the sport.

## --------Slow 'Em Down

The NASCAR Winston Cup Series engine's greater horsepower results in higher speeds, except at Daytona International Speedway and Talladega Superspeedway, which, as mentioned above, are the only tracks where NASCAR mandates the use of restrictor plates on the motors.

A restrictor plate is simply a flat metal device used to reduce the air-fuel mixture coming from the carburetor to the intake manifold, where it then flows to the engine's cylinders. The air-fuel mix produces horsepower; therefore, reducing that flow cuts both horsepower and speed.

Because of the restrictor plates and carburetors used on NASCAR Busch Series, Grand National Division racers, at times they can actually put out a little more horsepower than a NASCAR Winston Cup engine (approximately 425 horsepower for a NASCAR Busch Series motor to 415 for a Winston Cup engine).

The restrictor plates were first introduced in 1987 after veteran driver Bobby Allison's car went airborne at Talladega, taking down a couple hundred feet of the frontstretch catch fencing, spraying debris on the race fans seated in the front rows of the 2.66-mile superspeedway. Not too long afterward NASCAR officials decided that 200-plus mph speeds were too dangerous, and introduced the plates to slow the cars down at Talladega and Daytona.

NASCAR also has rules as to where the engines can be mounted in both NASCAR Busch Series, Grand National Division and NASCAR Winston Cup Series race cars, what kinds of metals can be used in the engine block (no aluminum blocks). NASCAR stipulates that all engine oil pans and coolers must be approved, and has minimum ground-clearance rules.

Those guidelines and more like them serve a purpose: They help ensure that competitors use stock parts where applicable, and prohibit illegal or unapproved parts, which helps maintain a level playing field.

But building these high-revving monsters ain't cheap—a standard NASCAR Busch Series, Grand National Division engine can run $30,000 or more, while a NASCAR Winston Cup Series motor can cost a race team $40,000 to $50,000 or more.

*It's not a part of the engine, but every race fan should be familiar with the term "dynamometer." It's a device used to measure an engine's horsepower, as well as test and monitor its overall performance. If you really want to impress your family, friends, and coworkers, you can call it a "dyno" for short.*

## --------How's It Handling?

Yet while the engine is a major component, the car's suspension system and how it's set up can literally mean the difference between winning the race and finishing way back in the pack.

The setup refers to the adjustments made to a car to help it handle on the racetrack. Among the elements considered in coming up with the right setup are tire pressure, shock absorbers, springs, weight distribution, and aerodynamics.

Yet the setup differs from track to track. For example, no matter how good a team's car works at Bristol Motor Speedway, a half-mile high-banked oval, the same setup would prove disastrous at a track like Talladega. The Bristol car, designed for a short track, is set up for frequent braking and responsive

cornering, while at Talladega drivers basically mash on the gas pedal all race long.
With the wide racing groove there, cornering
is less of a concern.

In addition to setups differing greatly
from one track to another, the teams are
also working with entirely different race
cars. Most teams, on both the NASCAR
Busch Series and the NASCAR Winston
Cup Series, have many different cars built
for the various tracks on the circuit. In
fact, most have at least five different cars
for the different tracks—a road course car
for a track like Watkins Glen International,
a short-track car for Bristol or Richmond
International Raceway, a flat-track car
for New Hampshire International Speedway, an intermediate speedway car for
a track like Charlotte Motor Speedway,
and a superspeedway car for Daytona
and Talladega.

Each car's setup is different for qualifying
and for the race itself. Crew chiefs and chassis specialists generally have a good idea of
the necessary changes, but often a completely different setup is required than in the
last visit to the track, depending on weather
and track conditions.

A key component in determining what's
needed is the driver himself, offering constant feedback to the crew chief and crew
during practice so changes can be made and
experimented with.

There are also little tricks that can be
used to alter the handling without doing
major work. For example, spring rubbers
can be removed or inserted into the
springs to improve the car's response, or a
little more air pressure can be added to the
car's Goodyear racing slicks to help the

tires heat up faster, or even a piece of tape
across a grill can help the car become
more aerodynamic.

Such little changes may mean only fractions of a second, but in NASCAR Busch
Series, Grand National Division racing, that
can be the difference between making the
race and having to pack your cars and equipment and going home.

The suspension isn't the most noticed
part of the race car, except when something
goes wrong. But the suspension components
serve a purpose—they help stabilize the car
on the racetrack.

Among the major components of a
NASCAR Busch Series, Grand National
Division car's suspension are the front and
rear coil springs, which support the weight
of the car; front and rear sway bars, which
help keep the car from excessive leaning in
the turns; shock absorbers, which soak up
the constant bumps and help keep all four
wheels planted firmly on the asphalt; upper
and lower A-frames, which connect the front
spindles, wheels, and brakes to the main
frame; and the spindles, wheel bearings, and
hubs, which hold the wheels on the car and
allow them to turn freely.

*Often, race fans will hear
announcers or crew chiefs talking about a
team adding or taking out a "round of
wedge" or a "round of bite" to their car.
This refers to the turning or adjusting of a
car's jacking screws found at each wheel.
This redistributes the car's weight at each
wheel, depending on which screws are
turned. If you've watched even one*

NASCAR Busch Series, Grand National Division race, you've probably noticed a crewman with a long ratchet-type wrench plug into a hole in the back of the car to adjust the bite. Those changes can help correct a "loose" race car—a car that feels like the rear wheels are going to spin out in the turns—as well as a "tight" race car, a situation where the front wheels don't want to behave.

## --------Putting the Power to the Ground

*The amount of air pressure in a tire is determined by the type of track on which it will be used. Teams will mark their tires by the speedway and what position that tire goes on the car.*

Another critical component often overlooked is the transmission and rear-end gearing. The transmissions used in NASCAR Busch Series, Grand National Division race cars are standard four-speed manual shift with a reverse gear, and they're vital for transferring the engine's horsepower to the rear end.

Having the proper gearing is also vital, and track size is the most important variable in determining the needed gear ratio. For example, a smaller track like Myrtle Beach Speedway would call for a gear ratio along the lines of 6.20 to 1, while superspeedways such as Daytona and Talladega would be closer to a 3-to-1 ratio.

The engine builder also has a lot of input, because he knows the rpm range his motors need to reach peak performance, and picking the right rear-end gearing is an important part of that setup. Choose the wrong gear and you either wind up with a blown motor or an engine that can't keep the rpms up going into and coming off the corners.

Either way, it's also the difference between winning and losing.

CHAPTER ELEVEN

# READY TO ROLL

It's time for the big race. Fans are packed into the grandstands, the infield, and living rooms across the United States. They're all ready to see some great racing action and are worried about nothing but the outcome only a few hours away.

But have you ever thought about all the hours of work that is done behind the scenes? Teams put in hundreds of hours of engine work, testing, painting, and body-work that the average fan never sees. All this work is necessary in order to secure a spot on the starting lineup for the next NASCAR Busch Series event.

There aren't many nine-to-five jobs on a race team. Teams work nonstop, even on their "off-days," to perfect their machines. All that effort comes to fruition on race day. When the green flag drops to start a NASCAR Busch Series, Grand National Division event, all the hard work and late

nights are forgotten. The teams are ready to race! This is what the teams have worked toward and they're anxious to see their efforts pay off.

Then, as soon as the race is over, the teams pack it up and start all over again.

## Slide It Right in There

Have you ever had to replace the engine in your car? Or even just do minor repairs on it? Then you know it's not an easy job, nor a quick one. But a NASCAR Busch Series, Grand National Division team can actually put a new motor in their car in a little more than an hour. And in emergency situations, they can do it in less time. That's fast by any measure, but these guys get lots of practice. From their arrival at the week-

*A race team often brings the equipment and parts necessary to the track to do most major (and minor) repairs to a race car. After an accident teams will work furiously to repair their cars in order to get a few more laps on the track.*

end's track to the end of the race, the teams have changed an engine or two.

Teams use a hydraulic engine hoist that helps them guide the engine into place. The hoist, which requires about six people to operate, raises the engine into place so the team can then bolt it to the chassis and get it race ready.

## --------Safety Is a Must

Going 190 mph around the racetrack in a tight group is a big part of NASCAR's attraction to the general public. But since NASCAR's beginnings fifty years ago, safety has been a primary concern. In fact, much of the NASCAR rule book is filled with recommendations to enhance safety.

Working around the fuel system and handling fuel during the weekend is one area where teams and NASCAR practice the most safety. The gas man on a team wears a fireproof suit and gloves during the servicing of the race car. NASCAR's rule book also contains several pages on this subject alone.

Some other safety rules that NASCAR requires are:

- A driver's seat must have a padded headrest and rib protectors. The seat must also have leg extensions on both sides.
- Drivers must also have a quick-release lap belt and a shoulder harness no less than three inches wide.

*Duct tape is a key element to the quick and temporary repair of any NASCAR race car.*

■ The roll bars in the car must be made of steel and any bars within reach of the driver have to be padded.

NASCAR, teams, and safety engineers are always working on new safety innovations, and they come along on a regular basis. As recently as the 1960s a race car driver's uniform consisted of blue jeans and a T-shirt. However, now each driver wears a fireproof uniform, gloves, boots, and a safety helmet.

Also in the 1960s, one of the more significant innovations was the use of the inner liner tires. An inner liner tire is basically a tire within a tire that helps the driver control his cars when a tire develops a leak on the track. Another safety innovation was a special fuel bladder which minimizes the risk of fire during accidents. Now all drivers also must carry a fire extinguisher inside their cars.

*NASCAR's history is almost a history of safety innovations. Many times after an accident, a new safety device would be designed to prevent such incidents in the future. For example, during the 1980s many cars became airborne while on the track. After losing control of their cars at high speeds, drivers would find themselves lifting off the ground. With the help of Embry-Riddle Aeronautical University, Roush Industries developed "roof flaps." The flaps, which are located at the rear of the roof line, pop up when a car spins around backward. This helps keep the car grounded.*

Safety innovations aren't limited to the race cars, though. Helmets, drivers' fire suits, even the retaining walls and catch fences at racetracks have all been refined and modified through the years to help in protecting the drivers. Rules such as the pit road speed limit and NASCAR penalties for sloppy pit work—loose tires on pit road, or parking with part of the car hanging outside of the pit box—have increased safety for pit workers as well.

## --------*Having a Backup Plan*

NASCAR Busch Series, Grand National Division teams hope they never need a second car at the racetrack. That would mean that the first car was damaged beyond repair and could not be raced. That's not a good way to start off the weekend. But just in case, most teams carry a primary car and a backup car to each event. Sometimes, however, a team with a smaller budget doesn't have the luxury of a backup car and must head home if they wreck their primary car.

A team's backup car can't be pulled out at will and substituted for the primary car, no matter how bad it is running. The backup car can only be swapped for a car that has been wrecked beyond repair. That determination must be made by the NASCAR Busch Series, Grand National Division director, not by a member of the team.

In fact, a secondary car cannot even be removed from the team's hauler without NASCAR's consent.

## --------The Sponsor Wants What?

**D**ue to the tremendous growth of the NASCAR Busch Series, more and more corporate sponsors are beginning to take note of the series. One of the most common ways for a company to get involved in the series is to sponsor a car. By doing so, the sponsor has a lot of say as to what the car will look like.

And the sponsor doesn't take decisions like that lightly—with so much money on the line, the company wants to get the maximum return on its investment. If they don't have an in-house design staff to do the job, most major sponsors will hire outside firms to come up with a logo and color scheme.

A sponsor has to consider many things beforehand, though. First of all, which brand in its product line is it marketing? Which segment of the fan base is it targeting? And most importantly, how can its logo be the most visible to the fans in the grandstands, as well as those at home watching their televisions?

Achieving the right combination of these variables can be a hard task. But there are many success stories. Ask a friend to name a car on the NASCAR Busch Series, and one of the first guesses may be the AC Delco

Chevrolet driven by Dale Earnhardt Jr. Recognition of the car is implemented by the sponsor's design on a sleek, clean, bright car—but the talent of the driver doesn't hurt either. Running in the top-five week after week and ultimately winning the championship is a sure way to get your sponsor's logo noticed.

## --------The Painter's Canvas

**T**ake a close look at the paint schemes of most of the cars on the NASCAR Busch Series circuit. You'll see intricately detailed designs that appear to take hours to complete. But not all of the design is actually paint. A large portion of the logos are decals that teams place over the paint job.

Each team's car must be freshly painted and decaled for the start of each weekend's event. To accomplish this feat, most teams have a couple of painters and bodyworkers on staff.

*Some larger corporate sponsors are also joining the ranks of the NASCAR Busch Series. In 1999, Pepsi partnered with Jeff Gordon and Ray Evernham to sponsor their joint effort in the series.*

A complete paint and decaling job takes from anywhere between two and three days, and costs between $2,000 and $3,000. The procedure for the job goes as follows:

First, the sheet metal is cleaned of any dirt, dust, or debris. Any amount of debris left on the car's surface will cause imperfections in the paint.

Next, the race car gets a coat of Bondo. Afterward, the Bondo must be sanded and the car pretaped.

Next, the car is sprayed with primer. The primer is used to give the paint a surface to adhere to.

Then, another round of sanding and retaping.

Now the car is finally ready to be painted.

Finally, the decals are applied.

Once the car is painted it can be "quick-cured" to allow the paint to dry quickly. Most larger teams have special paint booths within their shops that have heating systems to cure the paint quickly. The booths also have special ventilation systems to keep harmful paint fumes from reaching the workers and the environment.

*Many NASCAR Winston Cup Series teams have added increased costs to their paint and decal budgets in the last few years. Sponsors and teams have joined up in recent years to create special commemorative paint schemes for their cars. The schemes, designed to celebrate a special occasion or a product of the sponsor, have become very popular among competitors and fans alike. As more cor-*

*porate sponsors join the NASCAR Busch Series, don't be surprised if you see this trend carry over from the NASCAR Winston Cup Series.*

## Testing, Testing

For a team to be at their best on a race weekend they have to put in many hours of practice and testing. Testing is a critical part of the NASCAR Busch Series, Grand National Division, and teams squeeze it in whenever they can. Whether it's during the off-season, an off-week, or even on their way to the next race, teams will make time for testing.

The results of testing are varied with each team. Some teams use testing as a way to teach a rookie driver the different tracks that make up the schedule. Other teams use testing as a way to check a different setup or a new pit stop strategy, or to check their fuel mileage at a particular track. The teams are limited to seven test sessions each season, with each test to consist of no more than three days at one track.

*Adding to the rising costs of team ownership, testing can add a heavy punch to the yearly budget. Some team owners complain about the cost, unless they win at a track they tested on. However, NASCAR has made every effort possible to limit testing in order to create a level playing field for every NASCAR Busch Series team.*

CHAPTER TWELVE

# ON THE TRACK

ractice is done with, you've qualified for the race, and you've got the setup you want on your race car—now it's time to go racing.

You're strapped in the car, helmet on, waiting for that most recognized command in racing: "Gentlemen, start your engines!"

This is the moment that most drivers, crewmen, and race fans say gives them the biggest thrill—watching the green flag wave to start the race.

In every NASCAR Busch Series, Grand National Division race, the starting procedure is the same. The field pulls off pit road in two groups, the first eleven rows led off by one pace car, then the rest of the field pulling out behind another pace car.

The prerace warm-up laps are done this way to give every driver a fair chance at getting their tachometer readings set for the event's designated pit road speed. The two

pace cars will run at the pit road speed for a lap before the second pace car pulls off the track and allows the entire field to bunch up for the start of the race.

During those warm-up laps, the drivers also check the gauges of their race cars to make sure the engines are running at their peak performance, tighten up their safety harnesses, and begin weaving back and forth in an effort to warm up the Goodyear racing tires.

At the very start of the race, the field takes the green flag in a double-wide lineup, with the pole winner getting the choice of starting on the inside lane (the usual choice) or, in the case of some tracks like Darlington Raceway, where the outside groove is the fast line around, using the outside lane.

After that, however, the restart procedures vary, depending on circumstances.

Most caution-flag restarts in NASCAR Busch Series, Grand National Division events

ABOVE: All starts, and most restarts after cautions, are done double file. After a caution, the lapped cars will line up on the inside line.

LEFT: Some restarts are done single file. This happens when the leader has not lapped any cars yet, or when the race falls under NASCAR's "ten-lap rule."

OPPOSITE: In the case of rain a race must be postponed. However, if it begins to rain after a race has reached the halfway point, a winner can be determined.

are also made double file, with the lead-lap cars starting on the outside and the lapped cars on the inside. It is done that way to give the lapped cars a better chance of getting their laps back and possibly getting back in contention to win the race.

There are exceptions, though. If a caution flag comes out early and the leader has not begun lapping slower cars on the track, then the restart is done single file. Single file restarts are also used toward the end of the race under NASCAR's "ten-lap rule," which puts all the lead-lap cars ahead of the field should a caution flag result in the race going back to green with ten laps or less to go.

## --------When Is a Race Official?

So when is a NASCAR Busch Series, Grand National Division race considered an "official" event? It depends on the situation.

Under normal circumstances, the race is over when the "advertised distance" has been completed, according to the NASCAR rule book. That simply means that a race is over when the leading driver finishes the posted race length, whether it be 300 miles or 300 laps.

But what happens if a driver who is running first and has lapped everybody else two or three times is in an accident on the last lap? Then the driver running in second place, in order to win, has to keep going until he completes the advertised distance.

Sometimes, though, Mother Nature intervenes and shortens the race, whether it be because of rain, sleet, snow, or gloom of night. So what does NASCAR do when something like that happens?

If the race has reached its halfway point, no matter the length, then it is considered to be "official." That means the race can be halted and a race winner declared if the conditions that brought on shortening the race don't appear to be clearing up in a reasonable amount of time.

If the race has not reached its halfway point before being red-flagged, then the event isn't officially over. What NASCAR has done in those rare occasions is restart the race at the point it was halted at the next opportunity, whether it be a few hours later or the next day.

## --------Hey, Isn't He Running a Little Close?

One of the most stirring sights in NASCAR Busch Series, Grand National Division racing is the sight of forty-some race cars tucked in nose-to-tail as they race around the high-banked ovals at Daytona International Speedway and Talladega Superspeedway.

What race fans are witnessing when that happens is a real-time demonstration of "drafting," an aerodynamic effect that allows two or more cars to race together faster than a single car running alone.

While the science of the draft is complex, the explanation of the effect is simple. As aerodynamic as a modern-day NASCAR race car is, when it travels at high speed, it creates a slight vacuum around the rear bumper. A second driver, tucking the nose of his race car as close as possible to the rear bumper of the first car, can take advantage of

*Drafting is a technique drivers use on bigger speedways to increase their speeds.*

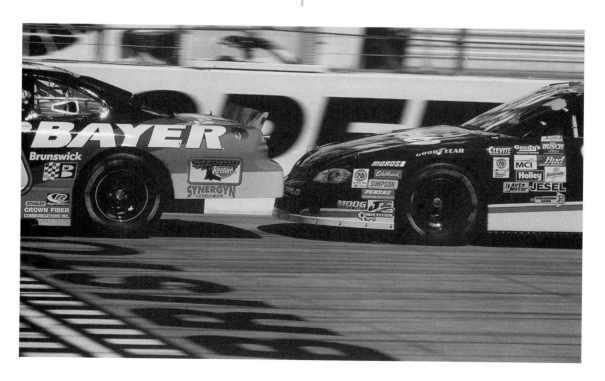

this by utilizing the reduced drag, thereby running faster.

The drafting effect works with more than two cars, too, creating the twenty-plus car drafts that are common at the NASCAR Busch Series, Grand National Division's two fastest race tracks.

Drafting also plays a role at other racetracks, such as Atlanta Motor Speedway, Charlotte Motor Speedway, Michigan Speedway, and the California Speedway, where lap speeds easily close on 180 mph.

## ‑‑‑‑‑‑‑‑*Eyes in the Sky*

Keeping a driver informed of what's going on out on the track is vital, and can spell the difference between avoiding an accident or not.

The two primary sources of information for a driver are his crew chief, who directs the crew from pit road, and his spotter, who has a bird's-eye view of the racetrack from his perch high above the grandstands.

Most of the time it's the spotter who communicates with the driver, warning him about approaching traffic, giving him the all-clear when he's passing someone, or even giving him the right line to take to avoid an upcoming accident.

The crew chief, on the other hand, keeps in touch with his driver to find out how the car's handling and what changes, if any, need to be made on their next pit stop. Some crew chiefs also call out lap times to their drivers, and serve as a sort of cheerleader, keeping him calm when the situation merits and pumping him up at other times.

While the rest of the crew also sport two-way radios hooked up to noise-reducing headsets and microphones, very seldom do they speak. Instead, the two-way hookup is to keep the crew appraised of what needs to be done on the next pit stop.

PART FOUR: *Pay Day*

CHAPTER THIRTEEN

# VICTORY LANE

# 13

The car running first completes the last lap and takes the checkered flag, meaning the race is over.

But while the rest of the NASCAR Busch Series, Grand National Division race teams begin packing up their cars and pit equipment, getting ready for the long haul back to their shops, the race winner's job has just begun.

The winner and his crew get to head for the big goal: victory lane! Of course, that's after he takes a victory lap around the track.

## --------Hey, They're With Us

But it's not just the winner and his team that will wind up in victory lane—a lot of other people head that way, too, filling the place to overflowing.

Just who are all these people?

News and magazine photographers, who are snapping away, trying to get the picture that will go across the nation and around the world.

The television network broadcasting the race is also there, and has "first rights" to the driver. They will either interview him while he's still sitting in his race car, or wait until he's climbed out and done a little celebrating with his jubilant crew. The choice usually depends on just who is broadcasting the race and how much airtime they have remaining.

In any case, when the driver climbs from his winning race car, more often than not he heads to the roof, waves to the crowd, splashes his waiting crew with Gatorade or some other handy beverage, then jumps down and hugs his wife or girlfriend.

That's usually the cue for the radio network's turn to interview the winner, as well as any local television stations that happen

*Victory lane often has a wild, excitable atmosphere in which drivers and crews can finally celebrate all their hard work.*

*Drivers usually take the time to celebrate before they're interviewed by network television and radio crews.*

to have wangled a pass into victory lane. Normally, the local TV stations have a special area set up, with the driver stepping over for interviews after the victory lane activities are concluded.

Once the network television and radio crews get what they need from the race winner, then it's time for him to face the photographers and begin the ceremonies. First, he gets his winner's trophy and check, usually presented by officials of the company that sponsored the race.

## --------The "Hat Dance"

After that, some special awards are usually presented to the winning crew chief and team owner—more often than not, a replica of the trophy the winning driver just received a few minutes earlier. Then the crew and guests of the team's sponsors (both the primary and associates) get to join in for some more photos.

Then comes the traditional "hat dance," in which the winning driver doffs hats representing each company that has something to do with providing the driver with the all-important funding that he and his team need to race.

One hat goes on...smile for the cameras...that hat goes off and another goes on...smile for the cameras...another hat off and another hat goes on—an action that will be repeated more than a dozen times during the victory lane ceremonies.

While the activities surrounding victory lane may seem like bedlam to most people, a driver who just won a NASCAR Busch Series, Grand National Division race doesn't mind, and the photos shot are very important to the sponsors.

Once the victory lane activities are over, and they usually take thirty minutes or more, the winning driver and sometimes his crew chief and car owner go to meet the print media for interviews.

The winning crew, however, gets to go back to work. Not only do some of them have to tear down and pack up all their pit equipment, but some members have to begin tearing down the car and engine for the required postrace inspection by NASCAR officials.

CHAPTER FOURTEEN

# THE NASCAR BUSCH SERIES CHAMPIONSHIP

When Anheuser-Busch stepped up to the plate in 1982 to sponsor NASCAR's newest touring series, little did anyone realize that they were hooking their wagon to what has become one of the nation's most popular racing series.

The NASCAR Busch Series, Grand National Division has soared in popularity since its inception seventeen years ago, and so has Anheuser-Busch's involvement in the series.

That first year, Anheuser-Busch kicked in $50,000 to the then-NASCAR Budweiser Late Model Sportsman Series, a huge number in those days to drivers who had been used to getting a few hundred dollars at most in postseason award money.

Since then, Anheuser-Busch's contribution to the NASCAR Busch Series, Grand National Division point fund has grown,

with its biggest increases coming in the past five years.

From that auspicious start in 1982, the postseason points fund grew to over $2 million in 1998, with Anheuser-Busch contributing $650,000.

In 1999 their part of the points fund grows even larger—$1.5 million, more than double their '98 contribution—which should push the total awards to more than $4 million once the NASCAR track point fund and other sponsor contributions are totaled in.

The top twenty finishers in the NASCAR Busch Series, Grand National Division final standings get to share in the postseason points fund, with most going to the series champion. In 1998 alone, Dale Earnhardt Jr. won more than $383,000 from the fund, which will push his season winnings well over $1 million.

*Dale Earnhardt Jr. celebrated this year's NASCAR Busch Series championship in grand style with his family. Left to right are his parents, Dale and Teresa, and his sister, Kelley.*

In 1999 the champion's share of the NASCAR Busch Series, Grand National Division points fund should be even bigger. With Anheuser-Busch's increased contributions, the champ should find himself richer by more than half a million dollars.

## --------How Is the Champion Determined?

To win the championship, a driver has to rack up the most points during the course of a season, set for 32 events in 1999.

Since NASCAR's inception, it has used a variety of point systems to determine its series champions, but the method the NASCAR Busch Series, Grand National Division uses has been in existence since 1975.

The point system is really quite simple. A driver earns 175 points for winning a race, with each of the next five drivers earning five fewer points. Thus, second place is worth 170 points, third is worth 165, fourth earns 160, fifth 155, and sixth gets 150.

The next five positions in the final rundown—finishing spots seven through eleven—are separated by four points per position, while everyone finishing lower than eleventh place is separated by three points per position. With a maximum of 43 starts per race, the 43rd-place finisher would receive 34 points.

NASCAR's scoring system also has provisions for awarding bonus points, but until recently the only bonus given was an additional five points to the race winner. That changed in 1997, when the NASCAR Busch Series, Grand National Division adopted the system used by its big brother, the NASCAR Winston Cup Series.

In that system, five bonus points are awarded to each driver who leads at least one lap during the course of a NASCAR Busch Series, Grand National Division event, with another five bonus points awarded to the driver who leads the most laps during the race.

A driver is considered to have led a lap when he crosses the scoring line in the lead. In theory, the number of drivers who collect a lap-leader bonus is limited only by the number of drivers competing in the race. In other words, if all 43 drivers in a given event led at least one lap, then all 43 would collect five bonus points.

As for the lap-leader bonus, it goes to the driver who leads the most laps. Sometimes that's the race winner, sometimes it's not. In fact, in the rare instances in which two drivers both lead the most laps, both earn five bonus points.

With the bonus points, a driver can earn a maximum of 185 points in a race—175 for winning the event, five more for leading at least one lap, and five more on top of that for leading the most laps.

For a driver to earn points in a NASCAR Busch Series, Grand National Division event, he must start the race and complete at least one lap. Sometimes, if a driver is sick or injured, he will be replaced by a relief driver, but usually not until he runs at least one lap

in the race. The relief driver can then run the rest of the race with the starting driver collecting the points.

At the end of the season, if two drivers tie in the point standings, the winner is determined by which driver has the most victories during the season. If neither driver has won a race, then the tie is broken by who has the most second-place finishes, and so on.

*In the NASCAR Busch Series, Grand National Division's seventeen-year history, thirteen different drivers can lay claim to having won the series championship: Jack Ingram, Sam Ard, Larry Pearson, Tommy Ellis, the late Rob Moroso, Chuck Bown, Bobby Labonte, Joe Nemechek, Steve Grissom, David Green, Johnny Benson Jr., Randy LaJoie, and Dale Earnhardt Jr.*

## --------When Do They Get the Big Prize?

In the series seventeen-year history, only three cities have hosted the NASCAR Busch Series, Grand National Division banquet: Charlotte, North Carolina, from 1982–94; Miami Beach, Florida, from 1995–97; and Beverly Hills, California, in 1998.

The black-tie formal dinner and banquet was held last year in the Grand Ballroom of the Regent Beverly Wilshire, with the top ten finishers in the NASCAR Busch Series, Grand National Division point standings receiving their bonus checks.

*Many special awards are received during the championship banquet, including the Clevite Engine Builder of the Year award.*

Other awards are also presented during the banquet, including the A. E. Clevite Engine Builder Award, which goes to the leading engine builder for the 1998 season; the Bill France Performance Cup, which goes to the leading auto manufacturer; the season-long Bud Pole Award; the Gatorade Front Runner Award; the Goody's Headache Powder Extra Strength Award; the MCI Fast Pace Award; the Raybestos Rookie of the Year Award; and the NASCAR Winston Cup Scene Most Popular Driver Award.

PART FIVE: *Off to the Racetrack*

CHAPTER FIFTEEN

**TAKE YOUR SEAT**

By the time you get to the speedway for qualifying and race day, the place is buzzing right along. From your spot in the grandstands it looks like there are thousands of people on the "other side of the fence." When the starter gets ready to wave the green flag to start the race, several hundred people are in the pit area and garage. So who is in charge of this crowd in the grandstands, infield, and competition area?

Simply put, the operators of the speedway are in charge, from selling tickets to making sure that your seat is ready for you when you get there, and not occupied by someone else. They advertise the event and provide parking and other customer amenities such as concession stands and rest rooms.

*Traffic control is critical at most racetracks. State, county, and local police are in charge of directing traffic on highways and roads leading into and out of the track. The speedway's own security force takes over directing traffic once it enters the speedway grounds. Also, track security is responsible for the race fan's safety, but they may call on the police when necessary. Once in the garage area, however, NASCAR officials are in charge, responsible for the pits and garage area as well as conducting the race itself. The NASCAR officials most visible to race fans are the flagmen in the flag stand, the pace car driver, and the inspectors who cover pit road. All of them take their orders from the director and other NASCAR Busch Series, Grand National Division officials, who are in the control tower.*

Basically, the races take place on three different types of tracks: road courses, short tracks, and speedways.

The only road course the NASCAR Busch Series, Grand National Division races on is Watkins Glen International, located in the Finger Lakes region of New York State. It's a closed course with lots of left- and right-hand turns, as well as short and long straightaways. Traditionally, all road course races are run in a clockwise direction.

A short track is an oval of less than a mile in length, measured from a certain distance away from the outside wall, while a speedway is anything that's at least one mile or longer. Speedway tracks are usually the fastest on the racing circuit.

On short tracks and speedways, one thing is common: NASCAR Busch Series, Grand National Division events held on them are always run in a counterclockwise direction. Just as no one seems to know why road races are run clockwise, nobody can explain why oval track races have always "turned left." Most racing historians say it's because early races were run on horse-racing tracks, which customarily ran counterclockwise.

*The NASCAR Busch Series races on a variety of racetracks, including short tracks, speedways, and road courses.*

*There are times when a team may use a car designed for a short track on an intermediate-size track, and even times when superspeedway chassis is the choice. This is because competitors in the NASCAR Busch Series, Grand National Division think in terms of chassis setup and horsepower.*

## --------At the Track

nce at the track, there are two main areas to watch the race: the infield and the grandstands. If you're among the first group, whether you arrive in a top-of-the-line motor home, a travel trailer, a converted school bus, or your family's old pickup truck, you will need to bring everything necessary for survival. However, some racetracks are making it easier for the fans watching from the infield, installing such amenities as shower rooms.

As for race fans sitting in the grand-stands, first, you'll want to dress properly. If you know it's going to be a hot, humid day, do not bring a parka or heavy jacket. On the other hand, if you're expecting a chill in the air, dress warmly and bring a

*A prime viewing spot for a NASCAR Busch Series race is near the start/finish line.*

blanket, cap, and gloves. To play it safe, always remember to check the weather forecast before you leave home (which is always available on NASCAR Online, just go to www.nascar.com).

Other items to bring if you have a grandstand ticket include (and this is just a partial list) a seat cushion, sunblock, sunglasses, a cap or visor, binoculars, earplugs, portable radio, a radio scanner with a list of driver/team frequencies, some sort of plastic tarp or rain gear in case Mother Nature decides to rain on the parade, and a cooler if permitted by the race track.

A note about coolers—most speedways do not allow coolers more than fourteen inches long, and track personnel check them for glass containers. So it's okay to bring your favorite canned beverage, but glass containers are forbidden. And as far as food goes, whatever turns you on!

There is also another type of race fan, who we'll call the "suite-heart." Did you ever wonder who gets to go into all those VIP suites above you while you're in the grandstands? They can be just about anybody—executives of sponsoring companies, their friends, friends of friends and customers, even good 'ol plain race fans.

Consider a sponsor of a contingency award—they may lease a suite for a season to entertain distributors, retailers, and potential customers. In reality, anyone with enough money, even an ordinary race fan, can rent a suite. Some tracks even have deals where you can rent part of a suite. Charlotte Motor Speedway pioneered the "speedway club" concept. They sell individual seats in suites to folks who may just want to sit in an air-conditioned suite and

be able to eat, drink, and make merry without having to spend thousands of dollars for a whole suite.

Whether you're watching the race from the infield, grandstands, or (lucky you) suites, minding your p's and q's is a necessity. Race-watching is supposed to be fun, and you have every right to enjoy yourself. Sure, go ahead and whoop, holler, and stand up in your seat—heck, everybody else does, so why not you? When your favorite driver is leading, yell, cheer and give your neighbor the old high-five.

But if your driver is having a bad day, don't take it out on the people sitting next to you, who may be cheering for somebody you don't like. They're at the racetrack to have fun too, and their idea of fun isn't having you describe their favorite driver in terms that would make a dockyard worker's face turn bright red.

*Just one simple word about throwing things: DON'T! Debris on the track is extremely dangerous to the drivers. Not only will you be thrown out of the racetrack, but possibly arrested too, since it's against the law in several states.*

## --------In the Garage Area

If you're fortunate to latch onto a pass that will get you into the garage area for a NASCAR Busch Series, Grand National Division race, there are a few rules and regulations you must follow.

For starters, dress appropriately. That means no open-toed sandals, cutoffs, shorts, and tank tops. Only long pants, shirts with sleeves (short or long), and regular street shoes are allowed. Alcoholic beverages are also prohibited. If you're part of a group tour of the garage area, stay with the group leader and watch where they walk because, like speedometers and fuel gauges, NASCAR Busch Series, Grand

*Drivers often take the time to stop and give autographs for patient fans.*

National Division race cars do not have horns! Remember, it *is* a garage.

**PIT STOP** *A quick word about autographs: Almost no driver, crew chief, or other team member will refuse to give you their John Hancock (or whatever their name is), but NASCAR frowns on autograph hounds in the garage area. Why? Because the guys are there to work and are thinking about one thing only: the race.*

CHAPTER SIXTEEN

## SOUVENIRS

16

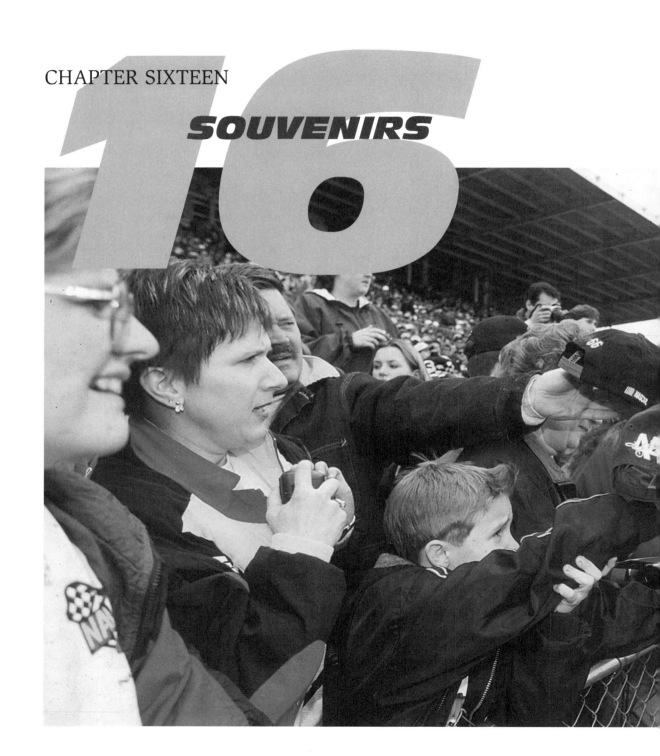

t's hard to believe that no more than twenty years ago souvenirs for race fans were few and far between. Since then, the racing souvenir and apparel business has exploded.

This is especially evident at the racetrack, where there are literally rows and rows of souvenir trailers, and almost every NASCAR Busch Series, Grand National Division driver, team, sponsor, and car make is represented. Caps, jackets, T-shirts, pullovers, watches, drinking glasses, beer mugs, bumper stickers, posters, race cards... there are tons of things a race fan can buy. You can spend as little as a few bucks or more than several hundred dollars, depending on the item.

Is there a lot of money to be made in souvenirs? Here's an example: A few years ago it was said that for every dollar seven-time NASCAR Winston Cup Series champion Dale Earnhardt made on the racetrack, he made ten more off it! Not every driver is as successful as Earnhardt—although his son, 1998 NASCAR Busch Series, Grand National Division champ Dale Earnhardt Jr., was among the top five of all NASCAR drivers in souvenir sales last year—but you get the point.

One thing's for sure, though. If a driver's line of merchandise isn't officially licensed or endorsed by him, then it's probably a bootleg. What's the problem with that? you ask. Simple: If it's a bootleg, it's probably made out of low-quality materials and won't last more than one or two trips through a washing machine. And who wants to buy merchandise that isn't authentic anyway?

CHAPTER SEVENTEEN

# HOMEWARD BOUND

Once the race winner has given his final interview and the NASCAR inspectors have finished their work, the race is *really* over. For the drivers, it's a trip home for a day or so—unless there's some kind of commitment between then and the next event. While not as prevalent as on the NASCAR Winston Cup Series, a growing number of NASCAR Busch Series, Grand National Division drivers have their own motor homes, so if their home isn't too far from the speedway, they use them to travel.

If the event is a little farther away, though, a growing number of NASCAR Busch Series drivers and team owners have private planes, which makes the constant traveling a lot easier. Most of the time, however, the drivers and teams use commercial airlines to get to the faraway events, or their

own passenger cars or team vans to drive to the races close to home.

The crew member that always uses the highways, at least thirty-two times a year, is the driver of the team's 18-wheel hauler. Once the truck is loaded with cars, parts, and other equipment needed to run a race, he usually tries to get out of the track as soon as possible. In most cases it's a long way back to the shop, and on the few races the NASCAR Busch Series, Grand National Division runs on the West Coast, a backup driver may be utilized to speed up the return journey.

Once they get back to the race shop, it's the truck driver's responsibility to see that the truck is unloaded, cleaned, checked, and then restocked with the myriad parts and supplies needed for the next race. That ranges from small parts like nuts and bolts

*As soon as the race is over, teams start preparing for the trip home. The team's hauler carries all the equipment and cars back to the shop and prepares for the next weekend's event.*

to larger items like spare engines, to extra cases of motor oil, lubricants, and cleaning supplies, even down to food, drinks, and snacks for the crew. The same routine is usually followed by NASCAR officials and inspectors. They leave the track as soon as possible—after inspecting the winner and top finishers, of course—and prepare for the upcoming event.

The team hauler has to be at the gate as soon as the track opens on the first day of the next event. (Usually it opens at six A.M., but some tracks hold check-in at twelve noon the day before practice is scheduled to begin.) The crewmen who are essential in making sure the car is ready for the driver have to be at the gate too. Their day usually ends at five P.M., when NASCAR officials issue the command, "The garage is closed for the day...pack up and we will see you tomorrow."

While not as prevalent as on the NASCAR Winston Cup Series, many of the people who work with NASCAR Busch Series, Grand National Division teams are "weekend warriors," part-time or volunteer crewmen who come in on the day of the race. They fill an important role in the success of a race team, with jobs that vary from as minor, such as setting up the pit area and equipment to packing

*Most often the only quiet time a driver has before a race is when he's completely strapped in to his race car.*

it back up after the race, to major, such as working on the race car during pit stops. While some teams pay to fly in these people, most of the part-timers spend their own money and time traveling from race to race.

Usually, the driver won't show up at the track until the first day of qualifying, whether the event has a single round or two rounds. Between races, and sometimes the morning before, drivers take care of things like television appearances, autograph sessions, sponsor commitments, and at times test sessions at other racetracks.

In fact, many drivers will tell you the time they most look forward to is the afternoon or evening of the race, whether the event is held on a Friday, Saturday, or Sunday. They can get into the race car, get a few minutes of peace and quiet, and prepare to do their jobs.

PART SIX: **A NASCAR Busch Series Directory**

# CHAPTER EIGHTEEN

# 18 NASCAR BUSCH SERIES TRACKS

Want to know where a track is located? Or have you been looking for tickets for your favorite track? Well, look no further! Here's a quick reference to all the tracks on the NASCAR Busch Series schedule, with addresses and phone numbers to put your search to an end.

## NASCAR Busch Series, Grand National Division Tracks

**Atlanta Motor Speedway**
P.O. Box 500
Hampton, GA 30228
Tickets: (770) 946-4211
Information: (770) 946-3950

**Bristol Motor Speedway**
P.O. Box 3966
Bristol, TN 37625
Tickets: (423) 764-1161
Information: (423) 764-3534

**California Speedway**
9300 Cherry Avenue
Fontana, CA 92335
Tickets: (800) 944-RACE
Information: (909) 429-5000

**Charlotte Motor Speedway**
P.O. Box 600
Concord, NC 28026-0600
Tickets: (704) 455-3200
Information: (704) 455-3209

**Darlington Raceway**
P.O. Box 500
Darlington, SC 29532
Tickets: (803) 395-8499
Information: (803) 395-8892

**Daytona International Speedway**
P.O. Box 2801
Daytona Beach, FL 32120-2801
Tickets: (904) 253-7223
Information: (904) 947-6800

**Dover Downs International Speedway**
P.O. Box 843
Dover, DE 19903
Tickets: (800) 441-RACE
Information: (302) 674-4600

**Gateway International Raceway**
P.O. Box 200
Madison, IL 62060-0200
Tickets: (888) 827-7333
Information: (618) 482-2400

**Indianapolis Raceway Park**
P.O. Box 34300
Indianapolis, IN 46234
Tickets: (800) 884-6472
Information: (317) 291-4090

**Las Vegas Motor Speedway**
7000 Las Vegas Boulevard North
Las Vegas, NV 89115
Tickets: (702) 644-4443
Information: (702) 644-4444

**Memphis Motorsports Park**
5500 Taylor Forge Road
Millington, TN 38053
Tickets & Information: (901) 358-7223

**Miami-Dade Homestead Motorsports Complex**
1 Speedway Boulevard
Homestead, FL 33035-1501
Tickets: (305) 230-7223
Information: (305) 230-5000

**Michigan Speedway**
12626 U.S. Highway 12
Brooklyn, MI 49230-1010
Tickets: (800) 354-1010
Information: (517) 592-6671

**The Milwaukee Mile**
7722 West Greenfield Avenue
West Allis, WI 53214
Tickets: (414) 453-8277
Information: (414) 453-5761

**Myrtle Beach Speedway**
4300 Highway 501
Myrtle Beach, SC 29577
Tickets & Information: (803) 236-0500

**Nashville Speedway USA**
P.O. Box 40307
Nashville, TN 37204
Tickets: (615) 255-9600
Information: (615) 726-1818

**Nazareth Speedway**
Highway 191
Nazareth, PA 18064
Tickets: (888) 629–7223
Information: (610) 759–8000

**New Hampshire International Speedway**
P.O. Box 7888
Loudon, NH 03301
Tickets & Information: (603) 783–4931

**North Carolina Speedway**
P.O. Box 500
Rockingham, NC 28379
Tickets: (910) 582–2861
Information: (910) 205–1299

**Pike's Peak International Raceway**
16650 Midway Ranch Road
Fountain, CO 80817
Tickets: (888) 306–7223
Information: (719) 382–7223

**Phoenix International Raceway**
P.O. Box 13088
Phoenix, AZ 85002
Tickets: (602) 252–2227
Information: (602) 252–3833

**Richmond International Raceway**
P.O. Box 9257
Richmond, VA 23222
Tickets & Information: (804) 345–7223

**South Boston Speedway**
P.O. Box 759
South Boston, VA 24592
Tickets & Information: (804) 572–4947

**Talladega Superspeedway**
P.O. Box 777
Talladega, AL 35160
Tickets: (205) 362–9064
Information: (205) 362–2261

**Texas Motor Speedway**
P.O. Box 500
Fort Worth, TX 76101–2500
Tickets: (817) 215–8500
Information: (817) 215–8520

**Watkins Glen International**
P.O. Box 500
Watkins Glen, NY 14891
Tickets: (607) 535–2481
Information: (607) 535–2486

CHAPTER NINETEEN

# CATCHING UP ON THE NEWS

kay, you couldn't make it out to the track for the big race, but don't worry, there's still another option. All NASCAR Busch Series, Grand National Division races are broadcast on TV and radio. Use the list below to find out what stations carry NASCAR events. There's also a handy guide to NASCAR's licensed publications and the fan clubs of all your favorite drivers.

## Television/ Radio Networks

### ABC Sports
47 West 66th Street
New York, NY 10023
Telephone: (212) 456–4867

### CBS Sports
51 West 52nd St.
30th Floor
New York, NY 10019
Telephone: (212) 975–4321

### ESPN/ESPN2
ESPN Plaza
935 Middle Street
Bristol, CT 06010
Telephone: (203) 585–2000

**FOX SportsNet/SpeedVision**
2 Stamford Plaza, 9th Floor
281 Tresser Blvd.
Stamford, CT 06910

**Motor Racing Network (MRN)**
1801 International Speedway Boulevard
Daytona Beach, FL 32114
Telephone: (904) 254–6760

**The Nashville Network (TNN)**
2806 Opryland Drive
Nashville, TN 37214
Telephone: (615) 889–6840

**NBC Sports**
30 Rockefeller Plaza
New York, NY 10112
Telephone: (212) 664–5313

**Performance Racing Network (PRN)**
P.O. Box 600
Concord, NC 28026–0600
Telephone: (704) 455–3228

**TBS Superstation**
One CNN Center
Atlanta, GA 30348
Telephone: (404) 827–1717

## NASCAR Licensed Television and Radio Shows

**Inside NASCAR**
TNN (television)

**Inside Winston Cup Racing**
SpeedVision (television)

**NASCAR Country**
Nationally syndicated radio show

**NASCAR Garage**
TNN (television)

**NASCAR Garage**
MRN (radio)

**NASCAR Live**
Radio show on more than 250 stations

**NASCAR Raceweek**
SpeedVision (television)

**NASCAR ShopTalk**
ESPN and ESPN2 (television)

**NASCAR 2day**
ESPN and ESPN2 (television)

**NASCAR Today**
Radio newscast on more than 300 stations

**This Week in NASCAR**
FOX Sports (television)

## Publications

**Inside NASCAR**
The Quarton Group
888 West Big Beaver
Suite 600
Troy, MI 48084
Telephone: (248) 362–7400

**NASCAR Preview and Press Guide**
UMI Publications
P.O. Box 30036
Charlotte, NC 28230–0036
Telephone: (704) 374–0420

**NASCAR Racing for Teens**
P.O. Box 588
Concord, NC 28025
Telephone: (704) 786–7132

**NASCAR Trucks**
Petersen Publishing
6420 Wilshire Boulevard
Los Angeles, CA 90048
Telephone: (213) 782–2000

**NASCAR Winston Cup Illustrated**
120 W. Morehead Street
Suite 320
Charlotte, NC 28202
Telephone: (704) 973–1300

**NASCAR Winston Cup Scene**
120 West Morehead Street
Suite 320
Charlotte, NC 28202
Telephone: (704) 973–1300

**Professional NASCAR Garage Magazine**
Babcox Publications
11 South Forge Street
Akron, OH 44304

## *Miscellaneous*

**Busch Series Grand National Ladies
Auxiliary**
P.O. Box 124
Davidson, NC 28036
Telephone: (804) 634–2127

**Motor Racing Outreach**
Smith Tower
Suite 336
Harrisburg, NC 28075
Telephone: (704) 455–3828

**NASCAR**
P.O. Box 2875
Daytona Beach, FL 32120
Telephone: (904) 253–0611

**NASCAR Online**
www.nascar.com

## *Fan Clubs*

**Glenn Allen Jr.**
7280 Jerry Drive
Westchester, OH 45069

**Blaise Alexander**
203 Performance Road
Mooresville, NC 28115

**Dave Blaney**
P.O. Box 470142
Tulsa, OK 74147–0142

**Todd Bodine**
P.O. Box 2427
Cornelius, NC 28031

**Mike Dillon**
P.O. Box 30414
Winston-Salem, NC 27130

**Dale Earnhardt Jr.**
P.O. Box 1298
Mooresville, NC 28115

**Tim Fedewa**
P.O. Box 609
Harrison, MI 48625

**Jeff Fuller**
P.O. Box 1435
Mooresville, NC 28115

**Mark Green**
2626 West Parrish Avenue, No. 121
Owensboro, KY 42301

**Bobby Hillin**
P.O. Box 561986
Charlotte, NC 28256–1986

**Lance Hooper**
P.O. Box 903323
Palmdale, CA 93590–3323

**Jason Keller**
P.O. Box 14748
Greenville, SC 29610

**Matt Kenseth**
10 Water Street-Rockdale
Cambridge, WI 53523

**Randy LaJoie**
P.O. Box 3478
Westport, CT 06880

**Curtis Markham**
433 Bostwick Lane
Gaithersburg, MD 20878

**Patty Moise & Elton Sawyer**
P.O. Box 77919
Greensboro, NC 27417

**Jeff Purvis**
900 Providence Road
Clarksville, TN 37042

**Hermie Sadler**
P.O. Box 871
Emporia, VA 23847

CHAPTER TWENTY

# YOUR NASCAR BUSCH SERIES GLOSSARY

Here is a glossary of terms and words unique to NASCAR Busch Series, Grand National Division racing.

**Aerodynamics:** As applied to racing, the study of airflow and the forces of resistance and pressure that result from the flow of air over, under, and around a moving car.

**A-frame:** Either upper or lower connecting suspension piece (in the shape of an A) locking the frame to the spindle.

**Air box:** Housing for the air cleaner that connects the air intake at the base of the windshield to the carburetor.

**Air filter:** Paper, gauze, or synthetic fiber element used to prevent dirt particles from entering the engine. Located in the air box.

**Air dam:** A metal strip that hangs beneath the front grill, often just inches from the ground. The air dam helps provide aerodynamic downforce at the front of the car.

**Alternator:** A belt-driven device mounted on the front of the engine that recharges the battery while the engine is running.

**A-post:** The post extending from the roof line to the base of the windshield on either side of the car.

**Apron:** The paved portion of a racetrack that separates the racing surface from the (usually unpaved) infield.

**Axle:** Rotating shafts connecting the rear differential gears to the rear wheels.

**Ball Joint:** A ball inside a socket that can turn and pivot in any direction. Used to allow the suspension to travel while the driver steers the car.

**Banking:** The sloping of a racetrack, particularly at a curve or corner, from the apron to the outside wall. Degree of banking refers to the height of a track's slope at its outside edge.

**Bear grease:** Slang term used to describe any patching material used to fill cracks and holes or smooth bumps on a track's surface. Can also be used as a sealer on the track.

**Bell housing:** A cover, shaped like a bell, that surrounds the flywheel/ clutch that connects the engine to the transmission.

**Bias-ply:** Layers of fabric within a tire that are woven in angles. Also used as a term to describe tires made in this manner. Last used in NASCAR Busch Series, Grand National Division racing in 1994.

**Binders:** Slang term for a race car's brakes.

**Bite:** (1) "Round of bite" describes the turning or adjusting of a car's jacking screws found at each wheel. "Weight jacking" distributes the car's weight at each wheel. (2) Adhesion of a tire to the track surface. See *Slick*.

**Bleeder valve:** A valve in the wheel used to reduce air pressure in tires. Bleeder valves are not approved for NASCAR Busch Series, Grand National Division racing.

**Blend line:** Line painted on the track near the apron and extending from the pit road exit into the first turn. When leaving the pits, a driver must stay below it to safely "blend" back into traffic.

**Blown motor:** Major-league engine failure, for instance, when a connecting rod goes through the engine block, producing a lot of smoke and steam.

**Bodywork:** The fabricated sheet metal that encloses the chassis.

**Bore:** Pistons travel up and down within each cylinder, or bore, in the engine block.

**B-post:** Post extending from the roof line to the base of window behind the driver's head.

**Brake caliper:** The part of the braking system that, when applied by the driver, clamps the brake disk/rotor to slow or stop the car. There is one on each wheel of a NASCAR Busch Series, Grand National Division car.

**Camber:** The amount a tire is tilted in or out from vertical. Described in degrees, either positive or negative.

**Camshaft:** A rotating shaft within the engine that opens and closes the intake and exhaust valves in the engine.

**Carburetor:** A device connected directly to the gas pedal and mounted on top of the intake manifold that controls the air-fuel mixture going to the engine.

**Chassis:** The steel structure or frame of the car.

***Chute:*** A racetrack straightaway.

***Compound:*** A formula or "recipe" of rubber composing a particular tire. Different tracks require different tire compounds. "Left-side" tires are considerably softer than "right-side" tires, and it's against the rules to run left sides on the right.

***Compression ratio:*** Amount that the air-fuel mixture is compressed as the piston reaches the top of the bore. The higher the compression, the more the horsepower.

***Contact patch:*** The portion of the tire that makes contact with the racing surface. The size of each tire's contact patch changes as the car is driven.

***Cowl:*** A removable metal scoop at the base of the windshield and rear of the hood that directs air into the air box.

***C-post:*** The post extending from the roof line of a race car to the base of the rear window to the top of the deck lid.

***Crankcase:*** The area of the engine block that houses the crankshaft.

***Crankshaft:*** The rotating shaft within the engine that delivers the power from the pistons to the flywheel, and from there to the transmission.

***Cubic-inch displacement:*** The size of the engine measured in cubic inches. The maximum size for a NASCAR Busch Series, Grand National Divisions engine is 358.000 cubic inches.

***Cylinder head:*** Made of aluminum, it is bolted to the top of each side of the engine block. Cylinder heads hold the valves and spark plugs. Passages through the heads make up the intake and exhaust ports.

***Deck lid:*** Slang for the trunk lid of a race car.

***Dirty air:*** Aerodynamic term for turbulent air currents caused by fast-moving cars that can cause a particular car to lose control.

***Donuts:*** Slang term for black, circular, dent-line marks on the side panels of stock cars, usually caused after rubbing against other cars at high speed.

***Downforce:*** A combination of aerodynamic and centrifugal forces. The more downforce, the more grip your car has. But more downforce also means more drag, which can rob a race car of speed.

***Draft:*** Slang term for the aerodynamic effect that allows two or more cars traveling nose-to-tail to run faster than a single car. When one car follows another closely, the one in front cuts through the air, providing a cleaner path through the air; that is, less resistance, for the car in back.

***Drafting:*** The practice of two or more cars, while racing, to run nose-to-tail, almost touching. The lead car, by displacing the air in front of it, creates a vacuum between its rear end and the nose of the following car, actually pulling the second car along with it.

**Drag:** The resistance a car experiences when passing through air at high speeds. A resisting force exerted on a car parallel to its airstream and opposite in direction to its motion.

**Driveshaft:** A steel tube, painted white under NASCAR Busch Series, Grand National Division rules, that connects the transmission of a race car to the rear end housing.

**Dyno:** Shortened term for "dynamometer," a machine used to measure an engine's horsepower.

**Engine block:** An iron casting from the manufacturer that envelops the crankshaft, connecting rods and pistons. Aluminum engine blocks are not allowed in NASCAR Busch Series, Grand National Division racing.

**Equalize:** Cars in NASCAR Busch Series, Grand National Division superspeedway races are required to run tires with both inner tubes and "inner liners," which are actually small tires inside the standard racing tire. When the inner liner loses air pressure and that pressure becomes the same as that within the outer tire, the tire is said to have equalized and a vibration is created.

**Esses:** Slang term for a series of acute left- and right-hand turns on a road course, one turn immediately following another.

**Fabricator:** A person who specializes in creating the sheet metal body of a NASCAR Busch Series, Grand National Division car. Most teams have at least one fabricator, and many employ two or more.

**Factory:** A term designating the "Big Three" auto manufacturers: General Motors (GM), Ford, and Chrysler. The "factory days" refer to periods in the 1950s and '60s when the manufacturers actively and openly provided sponsorship money and technical support to some race teams.

**Fan:** An electrically or mechanically driven device that is used to pull air through a radiator or oil cooler. Heat is transferred from the hot oil or water in the radiator to the moving air.

**Firewall:** A solid metal plate that separates the engine compartment from the driver's compartment of a race car.

**Flat-out:** Slang term for racing a car as fast as possible under given weather and track conditions.

**Flywheel:** A heavy metal rotating wheel that is part of the race car's clutch system, used to keep elements such as the crankshaft turning steadily.

**Four-barrel:** The type of carburetor used in NASCAR Busch Series, Grand National Division racing.

**Frame:** The metal "skeleton" or structure of a race car, on which the sheet metal of the car's body is formed. Also referred to as a "chassis."

**Front clip:** Beginning at the firewall, the frontmost section of a race car. Holds the engine and its associated electrical, lubricating, and cooling apparatus; and the braking, steering, and suspension mechanisms.

**Front steer:** A race car in which the steering components are located ahead of the front axle.

**Fuel:** Also known as "gasoline." NASCAR Busch Series, Grand National Division competitors use only 76 racing gasoline.

**Fuel cell:** A holding tank for a race car's supply of gasoline. Consists of a metal box that contains a flexible, tear-resistant bladder and foam baffling. A product of aerospace technology, it's designed to eliminate or minimize fuel spillage.

**Fuel pump:** A device that pumps fuel from the fuel cell through the fuel line into the carburetor.

**Gasket:** A thin material, made of paper, metal, silicone, or other synthetic materials, used as a seal between two similar machined metal surfaces such as cylinder heads and the engine block.

**Gauge:** An instrument, usually mounted on the dashboard, used to monitor engine conditions such as fuel pressure, oil pressure and temperature, water pressure and temperature, and RPM (revolutions per minute).

**Gears:** Circular, wheel-shaped parts with teeth along the edges. The interlocking of two of these mechanisms enables one to turn the other.

**Greenhouse:** The upper area of a race car that extends from the base of the windshield in the front, the tops of the doors on the sides, and the base of the rear window in the back. Includes all of the A, B and C pillars, the entire glass area, and the car's roof.

**Groove:** Slang term for the best route around a racetrack; the most efficient or quickest way around the track for a particular driver. The "high groove" takes a car closer to the outside wall for most of a lap, while the "low groove" takes a car closer to the apron than the outside wall. Road racers use the term "line." Drivers search for a fast groove, and that has been known to change depending on track and weather conditions.

**Happy Hour:** Slang term for the last official practice session held before a NASCAR Busch Series, Grand National Division race. Usually takes place the day before the race and after all qualifying sessions and support races have been staged.

**Harmonic balancer:** An element used to reduce vibration in the crankshaft.

**Handling:** Generally, a race car's performance while racing, qualifying, or practicing. How a car "handles" is determined by its tires, suspension geometry, aerodynamics, and other factors.

**Hauler:** The 18-wheel tractor-trailer rig that NASCAR Busch Series, Grand National Division teams use to transport two race cars, engines, tools, and support equipment to the racetracks. Cars are stowed in the top section, while the bottom floor is used for work space.

**Head wrench:** Slang term for a race team's crew chief.

***Horsepower:*** A measurement of mechanical or engine power. Measured in the amount of power it takes to move 33,000 pounds one foot in a minute. The engine of a NASCAR Busch Series, Grand National car can generally produce from 500 to 550 horsepower.

***Ignition:*** An electrical system used to ignite the air-fuel mixture in an internal combustion engine.

***Independent:*** Slang term for a driver or team owner who does not have financial backing from a major sponsor and must make do with secondhand equipment such as parts and tires. The term, like the breed, is becoming rarer every year.

***Intake manifold:*** A housing that directs the air-fuel mixture through the port openings in the cylinder heads.

***Intermediate track:*** Term describing a racetrack one mile or more, but less than two miles, in length. The NASCAR Busch Series, Grand National Division currently races on fourteen intermediate tracks: Atlanta Motor Speedway, Charlotte Motor Speedway, Dover Downs International Speedway, Darlington Raceway, Gateway International Raceway, Las Vegas Motor Speedway, Miami-Dade Homestead Motorsports Complex, Nazareth Speedway, New Hampshire International Speedway, North Carolina Speedway, Phoenix International Raceway, Pike's Peak International Raceway, Texas Motor Speedway, and The Milwaukee Mile.

***Interval:*** The time-distance between two cars. Referred to roughly in car lengths, or precisely in seconds.

***Jet:*** When air is sent at a high velocity through the carburetor, jets direct the fuel into the airstream. Jets are made slightly larger to make a richer mixture or slightly smaller to make a more lean mixture, depending on track and weather conditions.

***Lapped traffic:*** Cars that have completed at least one full lap less than the race leader.

***Lead lap:*** The lap that the race leader is currently on.

***Line:*** See *Groove*.

***Loose:*** Also known as "oversteer." When the rear tires of the car have trouble sticking in the corners. This causes the car to "fishtail" as the rear end swings outward during turns. A minor amount of this effect can be desirable on certain tracks.

***Loose stuff:*** Debris such as sand, pebbles, or small pieces of rubber that tend to collect on a track's apron or near the outside wall during a race.

***Lug nuts:*** Large nuts applied with a high-pressure air wrench to wheels during a pit stop to secure the tires in place. All NASCAR Busch Series, Grand National Division cars use five lug nuts on each wheel, and penalties are assessed if a team fails to put all five on during a pit stop.

***Magnaflux:*** Short for "magnetic particle inspection." A procedure for checking all ferrous (steel) parts (suspension pieces, connecting rods, cylinder heads, etc.) for cracks and other defects utilizing a solution of metal particles and fluorescent dye and a black light. Surface cracks will appear as red lines.

***Marbles:*** Excess rubber build-up above the upper groove on the racetrack. Also see *Loose stuff.*

***Neutral:*** A term drivers use when referring to how their car is handling. When a car is neither loose nor pushing (tight).

***Oil pump:*** This device pumps oil to lubricate all moving engine parts.

***P&G:*** Basically, the procedure for checking the cubic-inch displacement of an engine. The term comes from the manufacturer of the particular gauge used.

***Panhard bar:*** A lateral bar that keeps the rear tires centered within the body of the car. It connects to the frame on one side and the rear axle on the other. Also called a track bar.

***Piston:*** A circular element that moves up and down in the cylinder, compressing the air-fuel mixture in the top of the chamber, helping to produce horsepower.

***Pit road:*** The area where pit crews service the cars. Generally located along the front straightaway, but because of space limitations, some racetracks sport pit roads on both the front and back straightaways.

***Pit stall:*** The area along pit road that is designated for a particular team's use during pit stops. Each car stops in the team's stall before being serviced.

***Pole position:*** Slang term for the foremost position on the starting grid, awarded to the fastest qualifier.

***Post-entry (PE):*** A team or driver who submits an entry blank for a race after the deadline for submission has passed. A post-entry receives no NASCAR Busch Series, Grand National Division driver or team points.

***Push:*** See *Tight.*

***Quarter panel:*** The sheet metal on both sides of the car from the C-post to the rear bumper below the deck lid and above the wheel well.

***Rear clip:*** The section of a race car that begins at the base of the rear windshield and extends to the rear bumper. Contains the car's fuel cell and rear-suspension components.

***Rear-steer:*** A car in which the steering components are located behind the front axle.

***Restart:*** The waving of the green flag following a caution period.

**Restrictor plate:** A thin metal plate with four holes that restrict airflow from the carburetor into the engine. Used to reduce horsepower and keep speeds down. The restrictor plates are currently used at Daytona International Speedway and Talladega Superspeedway, the two biggest and fastest tracks raced on by NASCAR Busch Series, Grand National Division teams.

**Ride height:** The distance between the car's frame rails and the ground. On NASCAR Busch Series, Grand National Division cars, the minimum ride height requirements are five inches on the left side and six inches on the right side.

**RPM:** Short for revolutions per minute, a measurement of the speed of the engine's crankshaft.

**Roll cage:** The steel tubing inside the race car's interior. Designed to protect the driver from impacts or rollovers, the roll cage must meet strict NASCAR safety guidelines and are inspected regularly.

**Round:** Slang term for a way of making chassis adjustments utilizing the race car's springs. A wrench is inserted in a jack bolt attached to the springs, and is used to tighten or loosen the amount of play in the spring. This in turn can loosen or tighten up the handling of a race car.

**Scuffs:** Slang term for tires that have been used at least once and are saved for further racing. A lap or two is enough to "scuff" them in. Most often used in qualifying.

**Setup:** Slang term for the tuning and adjustments made to a race car's suspension before and during a race.

**Short track:** Racetracks that are less than a mile in length. Currently, the NASCAR Busch Series, Grand National Division holds nine events on seven short tracks: Bristol Motor Speedway, Indianapolis Raceway Park, Memphis Motorsports Park, Myrtle Beach Speedway, Nashville Speedway USA, Richmond International Raceway, and South Boston Speedway.

**Silly Season:** Slang for the period that begins during the latter part of the current season, wherein some teams announce driver, crew, and/or sponsor changes for the following year.

**Slick:** A track condition where, for a number of reasons, it's hard for a car's tires to adhere to the surface or get a good "bite." A slick racetrack is not necessarily wet or slippery because of oil, water, etc.

**Slingshot:** A maneuver in which a car following the leader in a draft suddenly steers around it, breaking the vacuum; this provides an extra burst of speed that allows the second car to take the lead. See *Drafting.*

**Splash 'n' Go:** A quick pit stop that involves nothing more than refueling the race car with the amount of fuel necessary to finish the race.

**Spoiler:** A metal blade attached to the rear deck lid of the car. It helps restrict airflow over the rear of the car, providing downforce and traction.

**Sponsor:** An individual or business establishment that financially supports a race driver, team, race, or series of races in return for advertising and marketing benefits. Usually, the sponsor's name, colors, and corporate or product logo are adorned on the race car for high visibility and product identification.

**Stagger:** The difference in size between the tires on the left and right sides of a car. Because of a tire's makeup, slight variations in circumference result. Stagger between right-side and left-side tires may range from less than a half inch to more than an inch. Stagger applies to only bias-ply tires and not to radials.

**Stick:** Slang term for tire traction, as in "the car's sticking to the track."

**Stickers:** Slang term for new tires. The name is derived from the manufacturer's stickers that are affixed to each new tire's contact surface.

**Stop 'n' Go:** A penalty, usually assessed for speeding on pit road or for unsafe driving. The car must be brought onto pit road at the appropriate speed and stopped for one full second in the team's pit stall before returning to the track.

**Superspeedway:** A racetrack of a mile or more in distance. Road courses are included. Racers refer to three types of oval tracks. Short tracks are under a mile, intermediate tracks are at least a mile but under two miles, and speedways are two miles and longer. The NASCAR Busch Series, Grand National Division currently races on fourteen intermediate tracks, four speedways (California Speedway, Daytona International Speedway, Michigan Speedway, and Talladega Superspeedway), and one road course (Watkins Glen International).

**Sway bar:** Sometimes called an "antiroll bar." Bar used to resist or counteract the rolling force of the car body through the turns.

**Template:** A device used to check the body shape and size, to ensure compliance with the rules. The template closely resembles the shape of the factory version of the car.

**That's Racin':** A catchall term usually uttered when describing an accident, mechanical problem, or just plain human error. Also referred to as "one of them deals."

**Tight:** Also known as "understeer." A car is said to be tight if the front wheels lose traction before the rear wheels do. A tight race car doesn't seem able to steer sharply enough through the turns. Instead, the front end continues out toward the wall.

***Tire rule:*** One of the few rules unique to the NASCAR Busch Series, Grand National Division, in order to hold down costs. It limits the number of sets of tires that can be changed during a race under a caution flag, with allowances made for tires flattened or damaged because of an accident. Penalties are imposed for exceeding the limits.

***Track bar:*** See *Panhard bar.*

***Trading paint:*** Slang term used to describe aggressive driving involving a lot of bumping and rubbing.

***Trailing arm:*** A rear suspension piece holding the rear axle firmly fore and aft yet allowing it to travel up and down.

***Tri-oval:*** A racetrack that has a "hump" or "fifth turn" in addition to the standard four corners. Not to be confused with a tri-angle-shaped speedway, which has only three distinct corners.

***200 mph tape:*** Also known as "racer's tape." Duct tape so strong it will hold a banged-up race car together long enough to finish a race.

***Victory lane:*** Sometimes called the "Winner's Circle." The spot on each race-track's infield where the race winner parks for the celebration.

***Wedge, round of:*** Adjusting the handling of the car by altering pressure on the rear springs.

***Wedge:*** Term that refers to the cross weight adjustment on a race car.

***Window net:*** A woven mesh that hangs across the driver's side window, to prevent the driver's head and limbs from being exposed during an accident.

***Wrench:*** Slang term for a racing mechanic.